Railroad Company Lehigh Valley

Lehigh Valley Railroad Co.

Railroad Company Lehigh Valley

Lehigh Valley Railroad Co.

ISBN/EAN: 9783744692809

Printed in Europe, USA, Canada, Australia, Japan

Cover: Foto ©ninafisch / pixelio.de

More available books at **www.hansebooks.com**

CHIEF ENGINEER'S OFFICE,
MAUCH CHUNK, Aug., 1852.

To the President and Directors of the Delaware,
Lehigh, Schuylkill & Susquehanna Railroad Co.

GENTLEMEN:

In pursuance with your instructions I have made a location and estimate for a railroad down the Valley of the Lehigh, from Mauch Chunk to a point on the eastern side of the Delaware River, opposite Easton.

From the southern terminus of the Beaver Meadow Railroad, opposite Mauch Chunk to Parryville—a distance of 6 miles—the route will occupy the old Beaver Meadow grade, portions of which will have to be raised and widened and other portions entirely renewed, having been swept away by the freshets, 1841, and subsequent washings. This part of the line will require about 30,000 dollars to put it in condition to receive the superstructure, exclusive of the bridges across the Lehigh River and Mahoning Creek. From Parryville to the Gap, a distance of 6 miles, the route crosses several sandy flats (in the aggregate about 2 miles) which vary from 1 to 15 feet below grade. The balance of the distance, 4 miles, it runs along the base of the Blue Mountains, which is very steep and abrupt, and is composed of red shale rock and gravel, excellent materials for the roadbed.

From the Gap to the head of Swartz's dam, a distance of 11 miles, the route crosses the slate formation, which in some places presents very abrupt and irregular points, rendering it rather expensive constructing the road. Sections 17, 18 and 19 include the heaviest portions. Sections 15, 16, 23 and 24 also pass over some precipitous bluffs. All the stone required for masonry upon this portion of the route will have to be transported from 1 to 5 miles. From this point to Allentown, a distance of 6 miles, the route crosses the limestone formation, some parts of the line pass valleys or flats requiring embankments, other portions elevated flats which need to be excavated, and steep bluffs of rock rising nearly perpendicular from the water's edge need deep cutting. From Allentown to Bethlehem, 5 miles, the route will occupy the site of the present public road a considerable portion of the distance; the rock upon this part of the line lies very near the surface and is of an excellent quality for building purposes. Quarries can be opened at a trifling cost, from which fine large stone may be procured for bridge abutments and other masonry requisite along the line. From Bethlehem to South Easton, a distance of 11 miles, the route crosses flats requiring embankments, along the slope of hills, &c., limestone bluffs to be excavated, and for a considerable distance along the public road, the location of which will make a change of its location necessary. Through South Easton the route has not been entirely determined upon; between the street and the canal, however, would seem to be the proper place. The limestone, sandstone and red shale occurring on the line furnish good and cheap materials for the construction of the road, and, with the exception of that part of the route traversed by the slate, wherever stone are required, they can be procured without much expense.

The location, though a preliminary one, is so near where the road must ultimately be made that I have based my estimate upon it. The limited time and assistance allotted me prevented my making a permanent location or taking such accurate measurements as I desired; yet as the line cannot be varied much the estimate will not be far from the true result. The curves may in some instances be eased at an additional cost, but generally where the sharp curve occurs there would be a large increase of expense incurred in making them much lighter owing to the steep, precipitous bank. The curves with one exception are short,—the longest on the route being 4,800 feet with a radius of 1,600 feet. The rest vary from 300 to 1,500 feet in length with radii of from 700 to 11,460 feet. Considerably more than half the distance will be in straight lines, varying from 500 feet to 1½ miles in length. The grades are very favorable—the descent in all cases (except the mile at South Easton) being in the direction of the trade. The maximum grade is 35.4 feet per mile and that for only 4,000 feet, and this may be reduced to 30 feet without great additional cost. The grades upon the ground do not occur in the order exhibited in the table, but are divided along the route, so that generally the light grade follows a heavy one. The grades are as follows:

Descending 35.40 ft. per mile for 0 miles 4,000 ft.
do	28.00	"	do	" 0	do	3,400 "
do	21.10	"	do	" 3	do	160 "
do	20.00	"	do	" 0	do	3,000 "
do	18.30	"	do	" 0	do	2,600 "
do	15.80	"	do	" 1	do	2,620 "
do	14.80	"	do	" 0	do	3,000 "
do	12.70	"	do	" 3	do	2,360 "
do	11.60	"	do	" 3	do	360 "
do	10.60	"	do	" 1	do	1,120 "
do	9.10	"	do	" 1	do	220 "
do	7.90	"	do	" 0	do	3,100 "
do	7.10	"	do	" 0	do	2,900 "
do	6.60	"	do	" 0	do	4,200 "
do	5.80	"	do	" 0	do	3,500 "
do	5.30	"	do	" 8	do	3,860 "
do	5.00	"	do	" 1	do	4,320 "
do	4.20	"	do	" 0	do	2,300 "
do	3.70	"	do	" 0	do	5,000 "
do	2.60	"	do	" 7	do	1,440 "
do	Level	"	do	" 6	do	1,020 "
Ascending	18.5	"	do			5,200 " through

South Easton to the Delaware River. This grade may be avoided by intersecting with the Trenton and Belvidere Road. The road is laid out for a single track 14 feet wide at the grade line on embankments, and 20 feet wide in common earth cuts. The slopes are generally one and a half in one, except in rock where they are 3 inches better per foot.

The bridges and culverts are all calculated for a double track and the bridge across the Delaware can be so constructed as to admit of four tracks, two of them on the top, 60 feet above the river, to intersect the Central Railroad, and two underneath to intersect the Trenton and Belvidere Railroad. The masonry and other mechanical work is intended to be plain and cheap, but strong and durable. The superstructure estimated has a rail of 65 pounds to the yard, laid upon cross ties 30 inches apart from centre to centre. The estimate of the grading, masonry (except the bridge abutment and piers), changing of public roads and grubbing and clearing, is 821,695 dollars. The estimate for the superstructure, including 4 miles of turnouts, frogs and switches is 375,000 dollars. The depots and other buildings necessary for the early use of the road I have estimated at 35,390 dollars. The total expenditure under these four heads amounts to 1,430,853 dollars, to which must be added the estimate for land and damages. This is a matter that cannot be arrived at with any degree of accuracy without consulting personally each property holder, which I have neither had the time nor opportunity of doing. I have, however, made an estimate of the probable amount of land that will be required for a double track, and affixed such a price as I think will not fail to secure it.

I place the amount at $100,000, which added to the items above enumerated makes the total $1,530,853. The prices are such as the work can be done for. I have averaged them as part of the work will cost less and part of it will probably cost more. In most places where embankment occurs there is not excavation sufficient to make it. The field work was commenced early in May (11th) and completed about the middle of June by our corps, under my immediate direction, since which time I have been engaged in the office making up the estimate which I now place before you.

All of which is very respectfully submitted.

ROBT. H. SAYRE,
Chief Engineer Delaware, Lehigh, Schuylkill
& Susquehanna Railroad.

LEHIGH VALLEY RAILROAD,
Office of the Superintendent and Engineer.

MAUCH CHUNK, Dec. 31, 1855.

To the President and Directors of the Lehigh Valley Railroad.

GENTLEMEN:

In presenting this my first report to you it may be proper to give a short account of the progress of the work under my charge from the date of my connection with it up to the present time. On the eleventh of May, 1852, I commenced the survey and preliminary location of the line from Mauch Chunk to Easton, and completed it in the latter part of June, after which nothing was done in the field until the work was let to Asa Packer, contractor. About the first of October I again engaged a corps and started upon the permanent location of the road which I completed during the fall and winter. In December Section No. 46, including the heavy rock cut through Mount Ida, opposite Easton, together with the masonry for the bridge across the river Delaware was sublet to Messrs. Atwood, Cook & Co. About the same time Sections No. 7 and 8, heavy rock cuts were let to Lentz & Bowman. In the same month the very heavy slate rock cutting was commenced by Mr. Packer, but under the immediate supervision and direction of Mr. Robt. Lockhart. Some of these cuts were over 100 feet in height and required a vast amount of labor to remove them. These heavy sections were let in advance of the balance of the work in order to complete the whole simultaneously. About the first of May, 1853, the residue of the line was sublet, and soon after the contractors generally commenced operations. The advance in the price of labor, provisions, &c., the scarcity of men and money and the great amount of sickness along the line the following summer, retarded the work very much. Many of the subcontractors had to have their prices raised to enable them to proceed with the work, some few abandoned their jobs which had to be relet, thereby causing much vexatious delay. After proceeding with the work upon Section No. 46 until the latter part of February, I was directed to change the original plan so as to form a connection with the Belvidere Delaware Railroad, as well as with the Central Railroad of New Jersey. This involved a very material increase of labor and expense, and delayed the completion of the work several months. Entire new plans had to be arranged and drawn, these required time to perfect, as the connection was a difficult one to make, on account of the difference in elevation and direction of the two roads. After the completion of the plans for the bridge across the Delaware, the work was sublet to Messrs. Comins & Murphy, who erected the span across the Delaware Canal, after which their contract was declared abandoned and the work relet to John W. Murphy. Much difficulty was experienced in the erection of the bridge across the river on account of frequent and continued high water. To obviate this difficulty it was suggested to try the experiment of raising the structure upon wire cables stretched from pier to pier. Mr. Murphy adopted the plan which proved eminently successful and enabled him to complete the work in a very satisfactory manner. The road was opened for the transportation of passengers from South Easton to Allentown on the eleventh of June, 1855, and two trains run daily to the latter place until the 12th of September, when the road was opened for travel to Mauch Chunk, one train a day being run until the 1st of October. Up to this time the road was operated by Mr. Packer, with rolling stock hired from the Central Railroad Company of New Jersey.

At a meeting of the Board of Managers held on the 19th of September it was resolved to accept the road for running from and after Monday the 24th inst. with the assent of the contractor. At the same meeting I was instructed to make arrangements with the Central Railroad Company of New Jersey for the running of the passenger trains upon your road, the time between the 19th and 24th being too short to perfect the running arrangements. I did not commence operating the road for the Company until the 1st of October, previous to which I contracted with the Central Railroad Company of New Jersey to run two passenger trains daily from Easton to Mauch Chunk, connecting with the Philadelphia trains on the Belvidere Delaware Railroad, thus affording ample facilities to the travelling public. On the 19th of November, one of the Central Railroad trains was withdrawn and a freight train with passenger car attached was substituted. This arrangement not proving at all satisfactory to the public, and having in the meantime purchased a passenger locomotive and cars, on the 24th of December the passenger train connecting with the early and late trains to and from New York and Philadelphia was run with our own cars; the Central Company still running the mid-day train. At the same time a daily freight train was put upon the road leaving Easton in the morning and returning in the evening. The receipts from passengers has been very satisfactory—in fact larger than was anticipated. The receipts from coal and miscellaneous freight has been limited by want of cars. The coal, iron and iron ore transported over the road has been in cars furnished by the Central Railroad Company, Beaver Meadow Railroad & Coal Company and Packer, Carter & Co.

In the early part of October an arrangement was entered into with Howard & Co. of Philadelphia to do the freighting business of the road (except coal, iron and iron ore) they furnishing cars, hands, &c., and paying at the rate of 3 cents per ton per mile for toll and transportation. An arrangement was also effected with A. D. Hope of New York for carrying his express matter at the rate of $150 per month.

Your road is now in excellent running order and I think will compare favorably with any new road in the country. There has been some interruption caused by slides upon the track, but nothing of a serious nature has occurred to interrupt the travel. No passenger train has been delayed over 4 hours since the opening of the road. The cost of maintenance of way has been greater than I anticipated owing partly to the materials used for ballast upon a portion of the track (slate gravel) crushing under the ties, but mainly to the continued and heavy rains of this fall and winter bringing down materials upon the track, rendering it necessary to employ a train and gang of men to keep it clear. There were several points along Kuntz' dam, where we cut through slate gravel lying upon the rock and notwithstanding the gravel was well sloped, the whole surface from the top of the hill has slid down, bringing trees, stumps, &c., with it. This material has had to be removed, and I have had it put upon the line of the second track, so that a portion of the amount charged to maintenance of way might with propriety be charged to construction.

The length of your road from Mauch Chunk to its eastern terminus is 45 38/53 miles. This, together with the Belvidere, Delaware connection and the various sidings, make about 48½ miles of single track. The main track is laid with a rail weighing 56 pounds per yard, supported upon cross-ties 6 x 7 inches and 7½ feet long, placed 2½ feet apart, and one-fourth of it is ballasted with stone or gravel. The road has a descending or level grade from Mauch Chunk to Easton, and with the exception of the curve at Mauch Chunk, has no curve of less than 700 feet radius. The sharpest of these curves may be improved by expending a considerable amount of money, but I doubt the propriety or necessity of doing this at present. When the contemplated connection with the Little Schuylkill is completed, thus forming the shortest route from Lake Erie to New York, it may become necessary in view of the increased rate of speed required to compete with other routes, to improve the heaviest curves. The masonry is all constructed for a double track road and is of the most permanent character. There is over a half mile of bridging upon the road, in length of spans varying from 30 to 183 feet. They are substantially built structures and are all arranged for two tracks. With this amount of wooden bridges upon the road you will perceive at a glance the constant risk you run of having the business interrupted by the destruction of one of them. The mere loss of the bridge itself would be nothing compared to the partial or total suspension of a large business. This liability to interruption will, I hope, induce you to give your early attention to the subject of replacing them with iron and stone structures as soon as the finances of the Company will admit of it. Most of the creek bridges can be rebuilt of stone, but it will be impracticable to build either of the river bridges of that material. Much prejudice has existed of late years against the use of iron in the construction of bridges but this has arisen, I think, from the fact of a number of iron bridges having failed. These failures, however, can probably all be traced to a want of knowledge shown in the plan and proportions of the structures. I have no doubt but that iron intelligently used is the best and cheapest building material we have where permanency is required; and since the success of that great work of art (the spanning of Niagara River with a wire suspension bridge), by Mr. Roebling, has been fully established, you need never be at a loss for the want of an imperishable material for your bridges. Temporary passenger depôts have been erected at Easton, Allentown and Mauch Chunk. At Bethlehem you occupy the house belonging to Mr. Packer, which makes a very good passenger house, and will probably answer your purpose for some time to come. You are using for passengers portions of the buildings erected by Howard & Co. for freight houses at Freemansburg, Catasauqua, Whitehall, Slatington and Lehighton. A permanent freight and passenger house is now in course of construction at Easton by the Central Railroad Company to be used jointly by the two roads. Platforms have been built at all the stations upon the road. A frame engine house for the accommodation of two engines has been erected at Mauch Chunk, and a temporary one to accommodate one engine has been built at Whitehall. A turntable has been put in at Mauch Chunk; water stations have been erected at Lehigh Gap, Whitehall, Allentown and Chain Dam, affording an ample supply of water, except between Allentown and Chain Dam, and at Easton. These points, especially the former, must be supplied previous to the opening of the spring business. Bethlehem would seem to be the proper point and I would recommend the erection there at once of a steam engine of sufficient capacity to pump water and saw wood. The President of the Thomas Iron Company has agreed to supply you with all the water you may want at Hokendauqua free of expense, provided you will make that place a passenger station. This I have assented to and ordered the water tank put up. Arrangements should be made at an early day for water at South Easton. We are now using the engine house and turntable of the Central Railroad Company at Phillipsburg, which they have kindly tendered to us, and probably an arrangement might be effected with them for its use for some time to come, but in the event of any accident occurring to the trestling or bridge between South Easton and Phillipsburg it would subject us to inconvenience and loss of time in running the engines backwards. I would, therefore, recommend the erection of engine house, car house and turntable at South Easton. There should also be an engine and car house erected at Mauch Chunk. Arrangements should be made as early as possible for the building of repair shops. The efficiency of our engines will be greatly impaired and the cost of transportation materially increased unless our rolling stock is kept in good order. Wood sheds should also be erected and two years' supply of wood purchased so as always to have one year's supply of seasoned fuel on hand.

Sidings have been put in at Mauch Chunk, Lehigh Gap, Slatington, Whitehall, Allentown, Bethlehem and South Easton. There should be several miles additional laid in the spring. There should also be a weigh scale put in at Mauch Chunk and some provision must be made for ground and sidings sufficient to make up the trains. Most of the coal operators in this region are expecting to increase their business, and several new works will go into operation during the spring and summer.

The connection of our road with that of the Belvidere Delaware Railroad provides a down grade or level road from the mines to tide water, over which coal can be transported as cheaply as by any other improvement now in use. The difficulty of the difference in gauge has been obviated by constructing cars with wheels of broad tread that run equally well on both roads. The connection with the Central of New Jersey Railroad provides a communication to Newark, Jersey City, &c., which is as short as that from any other coal region and with far more favorable grades, there being no opposing grade greater than 21 feet per mile.

The North Pennsylvania Railroad will probably be completed during the coming summer. This will open a new market to be supplied with coal and will also no doubt bring you a large amount of passenger and freight business.

The Morris Canal Company are constructing a branch from the eastern end of the Delaware bridge to their canal and are erecting conveniences for loading coal into their boats at that point, thereby saving them the risk and expense of ferrying their boats across the river and doubling their boating facilities without any increase of capital.

The Thomas Iron Company have constructed a branch from your road running into the bridge house of their furnaces, by means of which they unload their coal and iron ore where no handling is required, except to hoist it into their furnaces. This convenience of course gives our road the preference over any other improvement for supplying their works.

The Crane Iron Company have raised the bridge across the river to a level with our road and contemplate making a connection in the spring, with a view of getting a portion of the coal for the supply of their works by railroad.

The Lehigh Valley Iron Works, Allentown Iron Works and Lehigh Zinc Works situated in such close proximity to your road, and with excellent opportunities for unloading their coal and ore, must eventually get all their supplies by railroad.

With all these avenues open there can be no doubt but that upon the completion of the second track of the Beaver Meadow Road your road will be filled with business. In view of this, active measures should be taken at once to supply a sufficient amount of rolling stock to meets its requirements.

A survey has been completed of the route through Mahoning Valley to connect the Lehigh Valley and Little Schuylkill Railroads. The examinations develop a perfectly feasible route with small amount of curvature and no ascending grade coming east necessary. Total distance from the mouth of Mahoning Creek to Tamauqua 17 miles 250 feet. Length of tangents 14 miles 4,839 feet. Length of curved line 2 miles 691 feet. Total amount of curvature 412 degrees. Number of curves 13. Average degree of curvature 3° 15' or 1,763 feet radius. The maximum grade is 50 feet per mile and is in favor of the coal trade. A heavy cut is encountered at the summit (4 miles from Tamauqua) by coming out of the Schuylkill Valley with a level grade, but in view of the immense coal tonnage that must eventually pass over the road from the Schuylkill and Shamokin regions I would without hesitation recommend the level being preserved even at an increased cost. Upon further examination, however, I think this line will be found cheaper than one with ascending grades, from the fact of there being heavy embankments on each side of the cut, that would be materially increased by raising the grade. The general character of the work is heavy, the first four (4) miles after leaving Tamauqua is very heavy. The importance of the connection, however, would justify a large expenditure. I hope you will see the great importance of it, and have it put under contract immediately. Upon its completion and the completion of the Sunbury & Erie there will be a continuous line of railroad of uniform gauge from Lake Erie to Elizabethport, of less distance and far superior grades to any other route in operation or contemplation. The distance from Lake Erie to Philadelphia will be but 3 miles further via Lehigh Valley and North Pennsylvania than by the Little Schuylkill and Reading Railroads. This, I think, will secure to you at least one-half the travel to Philadelphia.

The Little Schuylkill Company have in contemplation the construction of a railroad commencing about $5\frac{1}{2}$ miles north of Tamauqua and running west about 6 miles into the Valley of the Mahanoy, from this point (10 miles east of Ashland) it may be necessary to make two roads, one opening the Mahanoy and the other the Shenandoah and Shamokin regions. In a communication recently received from J. Edward Barnes, Superintendent of Little Schuylkill Company, he says: "The first of these basins is about 15 miles long by $\frac{3}{4}$ wide. The second 20 miles long by 1 mile wide. The third is greater in extent than either of the other. The coal of these several basins is of excellent quality, easily and cheaply mined, and has a large advantage over many other regions from the fact of considerable portion of it being above water level. The capacity of these several coal fields is equal to at least 3,000,000 per annum, which would furnish business for several roads. New York is only 153 miles from the western terminus of the Mahanoy basin and 160 miles from the western terminus of the Shenandoah (in which is situated the celebrated Ashland mines), while a considerable portion of the Shamokin basin can be reached without exceeding that distance. The distance from these coal deposits is less to New York via Lehigh Valley and Little Schuylkill Railroads, and the grades and other natural obstacles less than by any other route. The only outlet at present for 500,000 tons of coal which they are prepared to mine in the Ashland district is the Mine Hill Road, whose acknowledged capacity is 1,000,000 tons per annum, but whose active business this year with *great effort* reached 125,000 tons. They surmount the Broad Mountain (which at Ashland is the southern boundary of the coal basin) with two planes, whose aggregate length is 9,000 feet and elevation 700 feet."

Tamauqua is some 7 miles nearer New York than the first mine reached by the Beaver Meadow Railroad, this will give them the advantage of about 20 cents per tòn in market over the Beaver Meadow region upon coal of the same quality and will, I think, induce a large shipment from that region.

RECEIPTS AND EXPENDITURES FOR 1855.

RECEIPTS.

	Coal.	Pass.	Frt.	Total.
October	$ 912 47	$6,812 93	$ 94 34	$ 7,819 74
November	2,648 42	6,223 44	590 03	9,461 89
December	1,792 43	5,675 44	1,768 45	9,236 32
				$26,517 95

EXPENSES.

October	$ 4,501 15	
November	5,350 60	
December	13,884 58	23,736 33
		$ 2,781 62

LEHIGH VALLEY RAILROAD,
Office of Superintendent and Engineer.

BETHLEHEM, Nov. 30, 1856.

To J. G. FELL, Esq.,
President Lehigh Valley Railroad Company.

DEAR SIR:

During the winter of 1855 I was instructed to contract for coal cars, but it was not until May that they began to come on and then very slowly. The first of January, 1856, your rolling stock consisted of one first class passenger engine, 4 first class freight engines and one fourth class engine, purchased from the Beaver Meadow Company for the repair and construction train, 4 passenger cars, 2 coal cars and 5 hand cars; yet with this discouraging state of affairs at the beginning of the year, at its close an amount of business was done over the road that must satisfy the expectations of its most sanguine friends, and should have the effect of placing its securities high in public favor. Owing to an inadequate supply of motive power and cars the coal business has been limited and has cost much more to do, than it would have done with a proper equipment. You have paid for motive power $11,883.69 and for car rent $15,720.36, both of these items are charged to coal transportation. The repairs of your locomotives have been large from two causes, both of which are in a fair way of being removed. The first has been the want of a shop of our own in which to do the necessary repairs, the latter and more fruitful source of trouble has been the overworking of your machinery, running the engines upon the road when they were totally unfit for service, because you had none to replace them with while being repaired; add to these causes you had one injured by the breaking down of the bridge at Easton, two injured in a collision, and have had to renew the furnace of the old engine purchased from the Beaver Meadow Company, these repairs amounting to over $3,500, should be classed as "extraordinary repairs."

ROAD-BED. The road-bed has been greatly improved during the past year, all the slopes that have caused trouble heretofore have been removed, the side ditches have been thoroughly opened, and the banks in many places widened.

TRACK. About one-fourth of the track is ballasted with broken stone and gravel, about ¾ of a mile of track between Lehigh Gap and Slatington and ½ mile above Lehigh Gap, which has always been troublesome and expensive to keep up, has been thoroughly ballasted with broken stone. 6.64 miles of second track and 1.16 miles of side track have been graded. In addition to this there are 4.5 miles of second track, including bridges and trestling and rock cuts, that were graded by the contractors in making the first track. There have been laid during the past year 4.5 miles of second track and 1.16 miles of sidings. The second track has been permanently laid with rails weighing 50 pounds per yard upon cross-ties 7 x 6 inches and 7½ feet long, placed 2 feet apart. The whole amount of track laid now is as follows: Main track, 45.72 miles. Second track, including Belvidere Delaware connection, 7.06 miles, sidings, 1.22 miles. 42 switches have been put in, 24 of which are in the main track and 18 in the second track and sidings. More track room is necessary at Mauch Chunk on which to make up the trains for the different roads. This seems to be indispensably necessary for the economical management of business. I would recommend the grading being done this winter so that it may be laid early in the spring. There should also be a half mile of track laid just above South Easton. This is all graded and would require but little expense to put it in condition to receive the rails. The track has been throughout the year and is now in in excellent order, no accident of any kind having occurred from any defect in it.

BRIDGES. There is over half a mile of truss bridges, and a like amount of trestling upon your road, all of which is now in good order. In the month of August one span of 180 feet in length of the bridge at Easton connecting the Lehigh Valley with the Central Road broke down while two locomotives were passing over it. Workmen had been adjusting the bridge a few days before, and probably screwed some of the rods a little tighter than others thus throwing an undue strain upon a few. Some of these proving defective in the welds gave way and as the whole vitality of the structure depended upon the rods it fell when they broke. The catastrophe was no doubt hastened by passing two heavy locomotives over together, yet it would eventually have given way, with the ordinary trains crossing upon it. There were seven men upon the engines at the time, all of whom escaped without serious injury except one of the firemen, who was drowned, having fallen into the Morris Canal, and being held down by some part of the machinery. One of the engineers fell the entire distance, over 60 feet into the canal amid the broken timber and machinery, yet, strange to say, escaped with but slight injury. This span of the bridge being over the Belvidere Delaware Railroad and Morris Canal, the fall of it obstructed both those improvements until the wreck could be removed, which occupied 4 days in doing. The connection with Belvidere Delaware Railroad remained unbroken so that the coal business was not unfavorably affected. Passengers were run across on the lower track until the connection with the Central Railroad was completed, which was accomplished in 23 days. Since this accident nearly all the bridges on the line have been very materially strengthened by the introduction of additional rods and braces. A competent man, Wm. Kellogg, has been employed, whose business it is to examine and keep them in thorough repair. The bridge over the Delaware should be covered as soon as the weather will permit, also that across the Lehigh at Mauch Chunk, across the Little Lehigh at Allentown and across the Saucon at Shimersville. The water stations are in good condition on the entire line of the road and afford at all times an abundant supply of water. There have been erected this year, one at Parryville, one at the Gap, one at Hockendauqua and one at Bethlehem, there is also one in the course of construction at South Easton shops. The station at Bethlehem is supplied by pumping from the river by horse power. I would recommend the erection of a small stationary engine at this point to pump water and saw wood. The Hokendauqua station is supplied with hot water from the furnaces. At South Easton the water will be pumped from the canal by the shop power. All the other stations are supplied from running streams or springs.

STATION HOUSES. There has been a passenger and freight house erected at Easton by the Central Railroad Company on your ground to be used jointly by the two Companies. At Freemansburg, Catasauqua, Whitehall, Slatington and Mauch Chunk you are occupying a portion of the buildings erected by the Howard Express Company. At Bethlehem you are occupying the brick dwelling belonging to Mr. Packer, at Allentown a temporary building erected by the Company. At Laury's, Rockdale, Lehigh Gap and Weissport you occupy buildings erected by the owners of property at those points. In view of the completion of the North Pennsylvania Railroad and its connections with your road at Bethlehem I would recommend the erection of suitable station buildings, for the use of both Companies. At Allentown it is highly necessary that better accommodations be provided for the travelling public. The present buildings are too small and totally unfit for the purpose. There should also be a passenger house built at Catasauqua and Hokendauqua.

ENGINE HOUSE AND SHOPS. These buildings are so far completed as to enable us to house 4 locomotives with shop room sufficient to do the repairs for a year or two to come. The stationary engine and necessary tools have been contracted for, and by the 15th of January the shop will be in operation. It is designed to complete accommodations for 5 more locomotives this winter. If additional motive power is purchased in the spring it will be necessary to extend the building. A blacksmith shop and shop for the repairs of coal cars has been fitted up at this point. There is a frame engine house erected at Mauch Chunk that accommodates two locomotives; this is insufficient for the requirements of the business, besides being very insecure. In conclusion, I would say that although from want of sufficient equipment our business has not been done as systematically as I would desire, yet in point of economy and freedom from accident I think it will compare favorably with most roads. Our passenger trains have sometimes failed from unavoidable causes to make the connections with our connecting lines, yet throughout the severe weather of last winter and the heavy slides in the spring, there has been but one day that the usual number of trips were not made over the road. Under the care of an overruling Providence we have been remarkably exempt from accident. No passenger having been injured in the least. There has been but one passenger car off the track, and that was caused by the breaking of a tender axle.

*ANNUAL REPORT OF THE LEHIGH VALLEY RAILROAD COMPANY.

The Directors of The Lehigh Valley Railroad Company present to the Stockholders the following report, for the year ending Nov. 30th, 1857:

The Lehigh Valley is mainly a coal carrying road; more than 75 per cent. of its receipts being derived from the transportation of that article.

The whole amount carried over the road during the past year, was 418,235 tons, and was distributed as follows:

To the Belvidere Delaware Railroad..........	121,648	tons
" " Central Railroad of New Jersey......	82,102	"
" " North Pennsylvania Railroad.........	43,239	"
" " Morris Canal	14,023	"
Delivered on the line of the road.............	157,223	"
Total	418,235	tons

Equal to 342,970 tons transported over the whole length of the road, at a cost of 39.7 cents per ton.

During the same period there were carried 128,158 passengers, equal to 42,627 over the whole length of the road, at a cost of 60.7 cents per passenger.

The following is a statement of the ordinary receipts and expenditures:

RECEIPTS.

To Coal Transportation	$337,074 62
Passenger do	70,786 05
Miscellaneous freight	29,280 96
Mail	4,045 83
Total	$441,187 46

---

* This is copy of printed report presented to the Stockholders by order of the Board of Directors, by the President. The Superintendent's original report, of which this is a short extract, has been mislaid and cannot be found.

EXPENDITURES.

For Coal Transportation	$136,304 67	
" Passenger do	25,896 66	
" Miscellaneous freight	10,106 27	
" Mail	154 99	172,462 59
Balance Net Earnings		$268,724 87

Against which has been charged:

Interest on bonds	$76,710 00	
" " floating debt	34,418 51	
Salaries of President and Treasurer and Expenses of Philad'a Office	8,928 98	120,057 49
Leaving a Credit balance of		$148,667 38

It is proposed to credit the dividend account with $107,670, being six per cent. upon the amount of stock issued; and the balance, $40,997.38, to the contingent account, against which will be charged the future purchases of iron and materials necessary to maintain the work.

The road having been in operation but two years, the officers have not learned from actual experience, the average deterioration of the superstructure and machinery, but the above amount is a very large allowance for that object.

During the year there has been

Expended	upon	Construction	$98,892 12
"	"	Machine Shops	6,000 00
"	"	Telegraph line	2,440 00
"	"	Real Estate	2,847 80
"	"	Locomotives	47,250 00
"	"	Cars	104,477 96

There are laid and in use 57.8 miles of track, as follows:— 45.72 miles of main track, and 12 miles of second track and sidings. There are also 8 miles of grading ready to lay, making nearly one-half of the whole road graded for a double track.

The plan pursued by the Company, of gradually pushing out

the double track, will, in the course of a few years, secure its completion; the excavations, bridging and masonry being calculated for a double track.

The equipment of the road consists of 15 locomotive engines, 6 passenger and 2 baggage cars, 504 five-ton, and 305 ten-ton coal cars, besides 61 platform, gravel, ore and hand cars, equal to the transportation of 500,000 tons of coal, with the estimated passenger and merchandise business. The engine houses, water stations and shops, are sufficient for the business of the year, and it is the purpose of the Board to limit the expenditure to the ordinary repairs. If this purpose is rigidly adhered to, and the business of the year proves equal to the last, the Company will be enabled to liquidate the entire floating debt. Though the amount of this debt is not large, yet such is the distrust of the public in regard to railroad securities, that the Board have had to submit to the dictation of rates of interest, which the ability of the Company for ultimate payment ought to have secured them from. We have also had the mortification to see our bonds linger at prices much below their value, when compared with other securities upon the market. The first and only mortgage upon the road is for 1,500,000 dollars. The interest has been punctually paid out of the earnings, leaving for the stock during the past year six per cent., with a large contingent fund. That bonds of this class should command but 65 per cent. at this time, is an indication that capitalists have not informed themselves of their real value.

The peculiar location of the road is such as to command a large trade with the least outlay of capital. At Mauch Chunk it connects with the Beaver Meadow Road, by which it has access to the extensive and rapidly developing coal fields of the Upper Lehigh. The success of the Beaver Meadow Railroad, now paying 10 per cent. per annum on its stock, is some assurance what the Lehigh Valley may do in a short time. At Bethlehem, we connect with the North Pennsylvania Railroad, and at Easton with the Belvidere Delaware and Central Railroads of New Jersey, thus giving us the benefit of three commanding outlets, all competing for the trade of our road, and saving us from the cost of expensive terminal arrangements.

The Fogelsville Railroad, extending from Catasauqua to Fogelsville, in Lehigh County, was completed during the past year. This road was constructed for the purpose of affording a supply of iron ore to the various furnaces along the line of the Lehigh Valley Road. This trade, now of great magnitude and importance, is destined to a large annual increase, the Valley of the Lehigh possessing advantages for the production of iron unsurpassed by any locality in the United States.

GRADES. The grades of the Lehigh Valley Railroad are highly favorable, being an easy descent in the direction of the trade. As an evidence of this we will state the performance of two of our engines. During the six months from April to September, inclusive, the engine *"Catasauqua" ran 11,236 miles, and hauled 11,231 loaded, and 11,246 empty cars, of five tons each. In the month of July, the engine "Lehigh" made 26 round trips, with an average load of 535 tons of coal per day. These engines were built by Norris & Son, upon Phlegers patent for coal burners.

The Board have not aimed to increase their trade by a reduction of the rates below those of the Lehigh Canal, but have relied for their share upon the peculiar facilities which the road affords for a portion of the business; and we take the occasion to express our gratification with the harmony that exists between the two Companies.

It remains for us to say, that the Company are much indebted to the energy and devoted attention of their Superintendent, R. H. Sayre, and their Cashier, John P. Cox, and to the various officers under them, for the performance of their duties.

By order of the Board.

J. G. FELL, President.

Philadelphia, January 11, 1858.

---

* Blew up at Catasauqua, May 16th, 1862.

[Reprint from Letter Circular.]

ANNUAL REPORT

OF THE

LEHIGH VALLEY RAILROAD COMPANY.

The Directors of the Lehigh Valley Railroad Company present to the stockholders the following report, for the year ending November 30, 1858 :—
The amount of Coal transported over the road for the year, was 471,029 tons, and was distributed as follows:—

To the Belvidere Delaware Railroad,	96,141	tons.
" Central Railroad of New Jersey,	122,000	"
" North Pennsylvania Railroad,	66,123	"
" Catasauqua and Foglesville Railroad,	4,012	"
" Morris Canal,	5,870	"
Delivered on line of road,	176,883	"
Total,	471,029	"

Equal to 363,141 tons transported over the whole length of the road.

During the same period, there was carried 117,745 passengers, equal to 36,925 over the whole length of the road.

The following is a statement of the ordinary receipts and expenditures:

RECEIPTS.

For Coal transportation,		$338,800 05
Passenger "		55 387 45
Express and Mails,		5,679 47
Miscellaneous freight,		42,178 38
		$442,045 35

EXPENDITURES.

For Coal transportation,	$151,400 73	
Passenger and Express transportation,	27,881 57	
Mail and Freight "	15,391 46	
		194,673 76
Balance, net earnings,		$247,371 59

Against which has been charged:
Interest on Bonds,	$84,300 00	
Current interest,	16,939 22	
Salaries and office expenses,	6,760 00	
Dividend in December,	112,138 00	
		220,137 22

Leaving a credit balance of $27,234 37

Included in the ordinary expenditures as above stated, is the sum of $17,208.90, used for the purchase of railroad iron and other materials, and for the settlement of sundry claims for damages by fire, etc.

A portion of the iron was used for the construction of the double track, but as we had sufficient margin in our net receipts to cover it, we thought better to put it all into the current expenses, than to fall into the too common error of increasing the permanent accounts.

During the year, there has been

Charged to Construction,		$56,795 71
"	Machine Shops,	1,825 75
"	Telegraph Line,	1,295 86
"	Real Estate,	2,850 79
"	Car account,	2,025 00

The Telegraph line was completed and opened for use in the latter part of January. The advantages to railroad operations, from the use of this invention, are very great, especially on lines where there is not a continuous double track.

An engine-house was completed early in the year at Mauch Chunk, for the accommodation of four engines.

There has been laid during the year, 1 8-10 miles of siding; 11 switches put in the main and second track; 7½ miles main track thoroughly ballasted, and 1¾ miles of second track and sidings graded.

The repairs upon the upper sections of our road (27½ miles), laid originally with the Danville and English iron, have been much heavier than upon the remaining portion of the road, which was principally laid with Phœnixville iron. On the first named portion, 124 bars per mile have been repaired and renewed, while on the latter, but 34 bars per mile.

It will be necessary to make provision for rebuilding the bridges at Mauch Chunk, Allentown, Freemansburg and two spans of the bridge at Easton. It is believed that the present wooden structures should be replaced by iron, as being free from the liability to decay and the accidents of fire, and in the end more economical.

The Quakake Road, connecting the Beaver Meadow and Catawissa Roads, was opened during the Fall. Our road is thus brought into a connected line from New York and Philadelphia to Northern Pennsylvania and Western New York. If but a small portion of the anticipations of some are realized, the importance to our road, from being connected with the trade of those sections, can hardly be estimated.

The East Pennsylvania Railroad, connecting with our road at Allentown, and the Lebanon Valley at Reading, will be open for use early in the Spring.

The friends of that enterprise are confident that a large business in the transportation of live stock and other heavy articles, between the West and New York may be carried on over this route. Seventeen miles of our road will be used in this connection, and the trade is confidently relied upon to swell our annual revenue.

To prepare for the various increasing demands which will be made upon us, will necessarily call upon the Company to push forward without much delay, until completed, their second track, with the requisite stations, machine shops and appliances, besides procuring a running equipment commensurate with the business to be done.

The various competing lines from the different coal fields to tide-water, are struggling to secure a full share of this important trade. Whatever advantages may be secured for the present by any one of the lines, through spasmodic exertions or very low charges, will have to be yielded in the end, unless supported by the real advantages of favorable distance and grade, as compared with its competitors.

By a comparison on these points of the Lehigh Valley and its connections with other routes, it will be seen that we need not fear the ultimate result.

It remains for us to say that the Company are much indebted to their various officers, for the faithful and diligent discharge of their duties.

By order of the Board,

J. G. FELL, *President.*

Philadelphia, January 10, 1859.

LEHIGH VALLEY RAILROAD,
Office of the Superintendent and Engineer.

BETHLEHEM, Jan'y 4, 1859.

J. G. FELL, Esq.,
President Lehigh Valley Railroad.

DEAR SIR:

I herewith submit report of the business of the Lehigh Valley Railroad for fiscal year ending November 30, 1858.

The whole amount of coal carried over the road was 471,029 tons (being an increase of 52,794 tons over last year) and was distributed as follows:

To the Belvidere Delaware Railroad..........	96,141	tons
" " Central Railroad of New Jersey........	122,000	"
" " North Pennsylvania Railroad..........	66,123	"
" " Catasauqua & Fogelsville Railroad......	4,012	"
" " Morris Canal	5,870	"
Delivered on line of the road, including Phillipsburg, Cooper's Furnace, &c...............	176,883	"
Total	471,029	tons

Equal to 363,141 tons transported over the whole length of the road, at a cost of 41.2 cents per ton (2 more than last year). During the same period there were carried 117,745 passengers (being a decrease from last year of 10,143) equal to 36,925 over the whole length of the road at a cost of 75.5 per passenger (14.8 cents more than last year). The pig iron, iron ore, lime stone and miscellaneous freight has increased largely this year. The ore and lime stone have been transported by the Thomas Iron Company principally—we have received the tolls only. The following is a statement of the ordinary receipts and expenditures. In the latter is included all the iron, timber and labor for strengthening and protecting the bridges and trestlings. The masonry has been charged to construction.

RECEIPTS.

From Coal Transportation		$338,800 05
" Passenger do		55,387 45
" Express		3,379 47
" Mails		2,300 00
" Freight		42,178 38
		$442,045 35

EXPENDITURES.

For Coal Transportation	$151,400 73	
" Passenger and Express Transportation	27,881 57	
" Mail	92 50	
" Freight	15,298 96	$194,673 76
Balance Net Earnings		$247,371 59

Compared with last year the receipts from coal transportation show an increase of.............. $1,725 43
From passengers a decrease of................ 12,019 13
" freight an increase of................... 12,897 42
" mails a decrease of................... 1,745 83

The increased receipts from coal bears no proportion to the increased quantity transported, from the fact that the freight was reduced early in the season. The decreased receipts from passengers is attributable to three causes, viz.: The reduced amount received from express companies. The general prostration of business, and the fact that our trains have not been run so as to afford good accommodations to the local travel. The increased receipts from freight proceeds from the largely increased amount transported together with a new arrangement effected with Howard & Co. for doing the business. The decrease from mail has been owing to the receipts for service in 1856 being included in last year. It has been our custom to return the receipts of one month with the expenditures of the one preceding it. This was done as a matter of convenience. I thought proper to change the plan and have therefore in addition to the

LEHIGH VALLEY RAILROAD,
Office of the Superintendent and Engineer.

BETHLEHEM, Jan'y 4, 1859.

J. G. FELL, Esq.,
President Lehigh Valley Railroad.

DEAR SIR:

I herewith submit report of the business of the Lehigh Valley Railroad for fiscal year ending November 30, 1858.

The whole amount of coal carried over the road was 471,029 tons (being an increase of 52,794 tons over last year) and was distributed as follows:

To the Belvidere Delaware Railroad..........	96,141 tons
" " Central Railroad of New Jersey........	122,000 "
" " North Pennsylvania Railroad..........	66,123 "
" " Catasauqua & Fogelsville Railroad......	4,012 "
" " Morris Canal	5,870 "
Delivered on line of the road, including Phillipsburg, Cooper's Furnace, &c...............	176,883 "
Total	471,029 tons

Equal to 363,141 tons transported over the whole length of the road, at a cost of 41.2 cents per ton (2 more than last year). During the same period there were carried 117,745 passengers (being a decrease from last year of 10,143) equal to 36,925 over the whole length of the road at a cost of 75.5 per passenger (14.8 cents more than last year). The pig iron, iron ore, lime stone and miscellaneous freight has increased largely this year. The ore and lime stone have been transported by the Thomas Iron Company principally—we have received the tolls only. The following is a statement of the ordinary receipts and expenditures. In the latter is included all the iron, timber and labor for strengthening and protecting the bridges and trestlings. The masonry has been charged to construction.

Receipts.

From Coal Transportation	$338,800	05
" Passenger do	55,387	45
" Express	3,379	47
" Mails	2,300	00
" Freight	42,178	38
	$442,045	35

Expenditures.

For Coal Transportation	$151,400	73	
" Passenger and Express Transportation	27,881	57	
" Mail	92	50	
" Freight	15,298	96	$194,673 76

Balance Net Earnings	$247,371	59

Compared with last year the receipts from coal transportation show an increase of............ $1,725 43
From passengers a decrease of............... 12,019 13
" freight an increase of................... 12,897 42
" mails a decrease of................... 1,745 83

The increased receipts from coal bears no proportion to the increased quantity transported, from the fact that the freight was reduced early in the season. The decreased receipts from passengers is attributable to three causes, viz.: The reduced amount received from express companies. The general prostration of business, and the fact that our trains have not been run so as to afford good accommodations to the local travel. The increased receipts from freight proceeds from the largely increased amount transported together with a new arrangement effected with Howard & Co. for doing the business. The decrease from mail has been owing to the receipts for service in 1856 being included in last year. It has been our custom to return the receipts of one month with the expenditures of the one preceding it. This was done as a matter of convenience. I thought proper to change the plan and have therefore in addition to the expenditures for the 12 months ending October 31, added the pay rolls of November amounting to $6,713.47.

During the year there has been charged to construction $24,275.16. To machine shop $1,825.76. To telegraph $1,295.86. To real estate $2,851.79. To cars $2,025. The telegraph line was completed and opened for use in the latter part of January. An engine house was completed early in the year at Mauch Chunk for the accommodation of 4 engines. Another for the engine of the repair and construction train is very much needed about the middle of the road.

During the excessive dry weather of the past season it became necessary to increase our water tanks. Three large ones have been erected. One at South Easton, one at Hokendauqua and another at Rockdale. We will require another at the Gap and one near Slatington to insure us a full supply of water at all times. There have been laid during the past year 1.8 miles of sidings, 11 switches put in main and second track, 7.5 miles of main track thoroughly ballasted, and 1¾ miles of second track and sidings graded.

The repairs upon the four upper sections of our road, a distance of 27.5 miles, laid originally with Danville, Trenton and English iron, have been very much heavier than upon the remaining portion of the road, which was laid with Phoenixville iron principally. On the first named portion 124 bars per mile have been repaired and renewed. On the last named 34 bars per mile have been repaired and renewed.

An additional track will be wanted at Easton if any amount of coal is to be shipped via Delaware Division.

It would facilitate matters very much to have the second track completed from Mauch Chunk to Parryville, from Laury's to Catasauqua, and from Bethlehem to Freemansburg. If our business does not increase so as to make it absolutely necessary I think it would be good policy to do this work and it would insure more regularity in our trains, and enable us to run our heavy ones at a reduced rate of speed. Two of our small bridges, one of 15 the other of 20 feet span, have been replaced by substantial stone arches. It will be necessary to make provision for rebuilding the bridges at Mauch Chunk, Allentown, Freemansburg, and two spans at Easton. Suitable station houses are very much needed at Bethlehem, Allentown and Mauch Chunk. The question of stand room for loaded and empty cars at Mauch Chunk is one of importance. Considerable extra labor is required for the business we are now doing. How a largely increased business can be accommodated there remains to be seen. Suitable shops for the repairs of engines and cars should be erected. We are now using a part of our engine house at South Easton. It is too small and unfit for the amount of work to be done. We should have a convenient shop and more tools to do the repairs economically.

Our equipment has been increased but little. Six five-ton and four ten-ton cars have been added. We have always been short of motive power, which has been the principal cause of the large repairs put upon it. In addition to the two engines ordered we want another for the freight. This might be fitted up in our own shop by purchasing the frame and castings. The advantage of this arrangement would be that we would have an extra force that would be of service in case of extraordinary repairs. Our connections are increasing, and I trust the policy of our Board will be to cultivate and encourage trade from all and to offer reasonable facilities for the business we may derive from them. The travel and freight from the Quakake thus far has been light, but I am satisfied that it can be largely increased by pursuing a proper policy.

The East Pennsylvania Railroad Company will complete their road in the spring, forming a new and direct route between New York and the West. They will expect their passengers and freight to be transferred over our road without change of cars.

With the exception of the disaster caused by the breaking down of the Allentown Bridge we have been remarkably exempt from accident. No passenger travelling upon our road has been injured in the slightest.

My acknowledgments are due to my assistants for the economical, skillful and energetic manner in which they have performed the duties devolving upon them.

       Yours respectfully,
         ROBT. H. SAYRE,
         Superintendent and Engineer.

[Reprint from Letter Circular.]

ANNUAL REPORT

OF THE

LEHIGH VALLEY RAILROAD COMPANY

FOR THE YEAR ENDING NOVEMBER 30, 1859.

The Board of Directors of the Lehigh Valley Railroad Company present to the Stockholders the following Report of the operations of the Company for the year ending November 30, 1859.

Referring to the comprehensive Report of the Superintendent and Engineer, R. H. SAYRE, Esq., they do not deem it essential to refer to the details.

The chief business of the Road is the transportation of Anthracite Coal; 74½ per cent. of the entire receipts being derived from that source. The relation of the Lehigh Valley Road, therefore, to this great interest, is that which mainly engages the attention of its Stockholders. We do not mean to disregard the ordinary freight and passenger traffic; but while giving those departments all reasonable encouragement, the general arrangement and equipment of the work has reference to the heavy transportation of coal and iron.

The whole amount of coal transported over the Road was 577,651 tons, against 471,029 tons for the year 1858; being an increase of 106,622 tons, and was distributed as follows:

	1859.	1858.
To the Belvidere Del. R. R.,	131,152 tons.	96,141 tons.
" Central R. R. of N. Jersey,	182,222 "	122,000 "
" North Pennsylvania R. R.,	77,483 "	66,123 "
" East Pennsylvania R. R.,	3,579 "	"
" Catasauqua & F. R. R.,	4,384 "	4,012 "
" Morris Canal,	4,688 "	5,870 "
Delivered on line of Road,	174,143 "	176,883 "
Total,	577,651 "	471,029 "

It will be perceived that the increase is altogether from through coal, arising from the fact that our rates approximated nearer to competing rates than heretofore.

The following is a statement of the receipts and expenditures:

RECEIPTS.

From Coal Transportation,	$391,766 81
" Passengers, Express and Mail,	68,161 70
" Miscellaneous Freight,	65,937 97
	$525,866 48

EXPENDITURES.

For Coal Transportation,	$160,895 67	
" Passengers, Express and Mail,	28,085 76	
" Miscellaneous Freight,	22,991 07	
		211,972 50
Balance, Net Earnings,		313,893 98

Against which has been charged:

Interest on Bonds,	$85,020 00	
Current Interest,	8,257 86	
Salaries and Office Expenses,	6,259 40	
Dividend in December, being 6 per cent. per year, ending Nov. 30,	117,981 00	
		217,518 26
Leaving a Credit Balance of		$96,375 72

$62,797.06 of which has been used in new constructions during the year, and the balance applied to liquidating the debts of the Company.

Of the $1,500,000 authorized to be issued under the first and only mortgage of the Company, $83,000 still remain unsold. This amount has been kept as a reserve, in case of any extraordinary demand upon the resources of the Company.

They have been able to keep the floating debt within the limits represented by the ordinary purchases of materials for the maintenance of the work. This is very encouraging when we regard its rapid development.

During the year the East Pennsylvania Railroad was finished and put into use. This Road forms part of a line from New York to the West, and sanguine hopes are entertained by its builders that a share of the trade between those points will be carried over it. Seventeen miles of the Lehigh Valley Road will be used in this connection.

The business from the Quakake connection has produced to the Company a gross revenue of about twelve thousand dollars, which was earned without material increase of expenditure. Viewed in this light, the aid extended to that work may be regarded with favor.

The peculiar advantages of the valley of the Lehigh, for the production of iron, are becoming every day more apparent. The furnaces along the line of the Road make annually upwards of 150,000 tons of pig iron, at as low a cost as in any other location in the Union.

There is now being erected at Allentown a large Rolling Mill for the manufacture of railroad iron, which will no doubt be followed by others of similar character.

The remarkable position of the Lehigh Valley, in reference to the three great coal fields, with the New York and Eastern markets, is claiming the attention of all parties interested.

There is no question that the best outlet for a large portion of the Wyoming Valley is through Solomon's Gap, and thence to the Lehigh. Fifteen miles of railroad from Penn Haven to White Haven will give uninterrupted communication by rail from both Philadelphia and New York, thus giving an impetus to the trade heretofore unfelt.

Parties feeling a deep interest in that work have already taken steps towards its construction ; thus placing its early completion as a probable result.

The Lehigh Valley Railroad will be benefitted throughout its entire length by the filling up of this link.

The Lehigh Luzerne Railroad, connecting the Hazleton Road with the Black Creek Valley, was finished during the year, by which a large and valuable field of superior coal was opened to the market.

The feelings of the people of Schuylkill County, in regard to the value of the Lehigh Valley as an outlet, is evidenced by their earnest efforts to procure the completion of the East Mahanoy, Tamaqua and Lehighton, and Auburn and Allentown Railroads; all of which connect with the Lehigh Valley Railroad, and by it give to their respective regions the most direct route to New York.

The Delaware and Raritan Canal Company are now engaged in the erection of extensive facilities at Amboy for the transhipment of coal, which, when completed, will create additional inducements for trade to seek this direction to market.

The Central Railroad of New Jersey has increased its shipping capacity at Elizabethport to an extent that will meet the full requirements of the present trade in that direction.

The coal trade, after several seasons of depression, is now experiencing the invigorating effects of a healthy demand, and we do not entertain a doubt that as much trade will be offered to us as our equipments will accommodate.

Upon the whole, we congratulate our Stockholders upon the present position and future prospects of the work.

By order of the Board,

J. G. FELL, *President.*

Philadelphia, January 9, 1860.

LEHIGH VALLEY RAILROAD,
Office of the Superintendent and Engineer.

BETHLEHEM, Jan'y 4, 1860.

J. G. FELL, Esq.,
President Lehigh Valley Railroad.

DEAR SIR:

The following report of the business of The Lehigh Valley Railroad for the fiscal year ending November 30th, 1859, is respectfully submitted.

The whole amount of coal transported over the road was 577,651 tons, and was distributed as follows:

To the Belvidere Delaware Railroad.........	131,152 tons
" " Central Railroad of New Jersey.......	182,222 "
" " North Pennsylvania Railroad..........	77,483 "
" " East Pennsylvania do	3,579 "
" " Catasauqua and Fogelsville Railroad....	4,384 "
" " Morris Canal	4,688 "
Delivered on the line of the road.............	174,143 "
Total.....................	577,651 tons

Equal to 480,753 tons transported over the whole length of the road.

During the same period there were carried 126,672 passengers, equal to 41,981 over the whole length of the road.

The pig iron, iron ore, lime stone and miscellaneous freight show a large and satisfactory increase this year and amounts in the aggregate to 186,774 tons. The following is a statement of the ordinary receipts and expenditures:

RECEIPTS.

From Coal Transportation..................	$391,766 81
" Passenger, Express and Mail..........	68,161 70
" Freight	65,937 97
	$525,866 48

Expenditures.

For Coal Transportation	$160,896 07	
" Passenger, Express and Mail	28,085 76	
" Freight	22,991 07	211,972 90

Balance net earnings $313,893 58

Compared with last year the receipts from coal
transportation show an increase of $52,966 76
From passenger, mail and express transportation
    show an increase of 7,094 78
" freight transportation show an increase of .. 23,759 59

The number of miles run by coal and freight trains was 138,551, and the receipts per mile run were $3.30.

The number of miles run by passenger trains was 75,920, and the receipts per mile run were 89.7 cents.

Total mileage of all trains, including gravel trains, 241,439.

Average receipts from all sources per mile run were $2.18.

The cost per mile run, including all trains, 87.8 cents.

During the year there has been charged to construction:

For grading and masonry for new shops at South Easton	$ 9,418 72	
" labor on second track and sidings	12,318 25	
" railroad ties, chairs, spikes and frogs	5,470 00	
" old railroad iron used for second track and sidings and on hand	25,000 00	
" covering bridges	3,614 16	
" engine house and boarding house at Laury's	1,088 97	
" car shop, smith shop, passenger car house at Mauch Chunk	2,423 93	
" store house and new tank	381 34	
" connection at Delaware Canal basin	101 83	
" Masonry at Easton bridge and culverts	3,049 12	
Making a total of	$62,866 32	

There has been charged to machine shops (for tools and machinery) the sum of $4,834.93, and to real estate $1,259.97.

During the past year there have been 2.78 miles of second track and 2.17 miles of sidings laid. There are now in use (including the Belvidere Delaware Railroad connections) 13 miles of second track and 5.85 miles of sidings. Two miles of second track and nearly two miles of sidings have been graded, and there are now 10 miles of second track graded ready for the rails. One span of bridge of 130 feet and the trestling at the connection with the Belvidere Delaware Railroad has been removed and an embankment substituted. One span of 165 feet of the bridge connecting the Central Railroad with ours has been replaced by a substantial iron structure. The main bridge at Easton, those over Balliet's Creek, Trout Creek and Lizzard Creek have been enclosed and painted. One truss of 66 feet span across the public road near Easton, one of 35 feet span at Allentown and one of 37 feet span near Catasauqua have been rebuilt. There has been expended on bridges, exclusive of the iron one, $7,288.83. The necessary walls have been erected at Coplay Station to dispense with 670 feet lineal of trestling by substituting an embankment which we are now at work upon. We are also widening the rock cut at Easton with a view of dispensing with 600 feet lineal of trestling at that point. The grading of the grounds about the engine house and shops at South Easton is completed and the foundations laid for machine, boiler and blacksmith shops of sufficient dimensions to accommodate our repairs for a number of years. A stone building 138 by 36, two stories high, has been erected for the purpose of repairing and building cars. There has been expended in these improvements $9,418.72. There has been an engine house built at Laury's Station for the accommodation of the engine used on the construction and repair train.

There has also been a boarding house erected for the men engaged with the train. Extensive repairs have been made to the grist mill on our property at the mouth of Mahoning Creek, and a storehouse erected for receiving grain and shipping the products of the mill. At Mauch Chunk a shop was purchased and a blacksmith shop built for the repairs of coal cars. Our road equipment has been increased during the past year by the addition of two first class freight engines, two passenger engines (all coal burners), 100 eight wheel coal cars, two first class passenger cars and nine platform cars.

In anticipation of the increase of business next year, two first class freight engines have been ordered.

Lumber has been purchased for building 100 eight wheel cars and the necessary machinery is now being put in the shop at South Easton to enable us to build them.

Your attention is respectfully called to the necessity of providing suitable station houses at Bethlehem, Allentown, Catasauqua, Slatington and Mauch Chunk for the better accommodation of the public.

The business from the Quakake and East Pennsylvania Railroad has not been so large as was anticipated. It is steadily improving, however, and will in time, with a proper arrangement of trains add materially to our revenue. From the former we have received this year about $12,000, and from the latter (which was completed in May), about $8,474. The Ironton Railroad, connecting with us one mile above the Lehigh Valley Iron Works, and extending out to the ore district of North Whitehall, a distance of 5 miles, will be completed the present winter, and will bring considerable tonnage to our road. There is a large rolling mill in the course of erection at Allentown which will no doubt contribute largely to our local business.

The track has been kept in good order and our trains have run with a great degree of regularity. No accidents have occurred and but one serious interruption. This was occasioned by a severe freshet in the "Little Lehigh," which undermined the trestling at the mouth of the stream and caused a delay of our business of two days. To provide against a similar occurrence, there should be an iron bridge built over the stream at an early day. I trust the work of replacing our wooden structures with iron ones will go on vigorously and that the day is not remote when we will be released from all apprehensions of danger from decayed timbers, fire or freshet.

It is gratifying to again report the fidelity and zeal of our officers and employees generally.

Very respectfully yours,

ROBT. H. SAYRE,

Superintendent and Engineer.

LEHIGH VALLEY RAILROAD,
Office of Superintendent and Engineer.

BETHLEHEM, Nov. 30, 1860.

J. G. FELL, Esq.,
President Lehigh Valley Railroad Co.

DEAR SIR:

The following report of the business of the Lehigh Valley Railroad for the fiscal year ending November 30, 1860, is respectfully submitted. The whole amount of coal transportation over the road was 730,642 tons, and was distributed as follows:

	1860.	1859.
To the Belvidere Delaware Railroad..	146,931	131,152 tons
" " Central Railroad of N. J.....	271,262	182,222 "
" " North Penn. Railroad.......	91,327	77,484 "
" " East " "	11,030	3,579 "
" " Catasauqua & Fog. Railroad..	4,875	4,384 "
" " Ironton Railroad	463	—
" " Morris Canal	997	4,688 "
Delivered on the line of road........	203,757	174,143 "
Totals.............	730,642	577,652 tons

Equal to 618,585 tons transported over the whole length of the road.

During the same period there were carried 158,120½ passengers, equal to 48,167 over the whole length of the road. The pig iron, iron ore, lime stone and miscellaneous freight show a large and satisfactory increase this year, and amount in the aggregate to over 250,000 tons.

The following is a statement of the ordinary receipts and expenditures:

RECEIPTS.

From Coal Transportation	$514,530	40
" Passenger, Express and Mail	78,537	79
" Freight	86,840	40
	$679,908	59

EXPENDITURES.

For Coal Transportation	$258,408	68		
" Passenger, Express and Mail	41,523	09		
" Freight	37,937	28	337,869	05
			$342,039	54

Compared with last year the receipts from coal show an increase of	$122,763	59
From passenger, mail and express an increase of	10,376	09
From freight an increase of	20,902	43

The number of miles run by coal and freight trains was 183,500, and receipts per mile run $3.27. The number of miles run by passenger trains was 89,490, and the receipts per mile run 87.7 cents. Total mileage of all trains, including gravel and construction, 329,630. Receipts from all sources per mile run $2.06.

Included in the ordinary expenses as above stated are the following sums:

For the purchase of railroad iron	$38,206	15
" iron bridge at Easton	8,008	52
Widening rock cut at Easton	10,503	55
Embankments and masonry at Coplay	4,406	58
Iron turn-table at Mauch Chunk	1,354	12
Damages to persons and property	5,175	62
Loss of locomotive Excelsior, March 28, 1860	8,000	00

There has been charged to construction the following sums:

New shops, &c., at South Easton	$20,962	23
Car house at Mauch Chunk	1,540	26
Reservoir at South Easton	578	66
Passenger depôt at Allentown	4,165	50
Do and freight depôt at Catasauqua	932	04
Land at Glendon for side tracks	1,138	79
Railroad iron	11,420	40
Cross-ties	3,196	50
Chairs	807	55
Spikes	771	50
Second track and sidings	12,201	15
New water tanks, depôt at Mauch Chunk	2,533	21
	$60,247	79

There have been 2.6 miles of second track and 1 mile of siding laid, and there are now in use (including the Belvidere Delaware connection) 15.6 miles of second track and 6.7 miles of sidings. 3.2 miles of second track have been graded and there are now 10.6 miles ready for the ballast and track.

The road-bed has been much improved during the past year. The cut at Easton has been enlarged and about 600 lineal feet of trestling dispensed with. This was a tedious and expensive piece of work on account of the great care requisite to prevent interruption to the trains. Considerable progress has been made toward filling up the trestling above Easton Station. A third track which has been much needed for stand room is now being graded above our shops at South Easton. The grading for a third track at Bethlehem, long enough to stand 200 cars upon, is nearly completed. A double track embankment has been substituted for 670 feet of trestling at Coplay. The single track trestling at Lehigh Valley Furnace has been replaced by a substantial double track trestling. The side drains have all been cleaned out, and the material used for widening out the banks. The track is now in better condition than at any former period. Almost the entire length of it has been thoroughly ballasted with broken stone or gravel. 1,900 tons of new iron has been used in repairs, together with 10,643 new chairs and 34,668 cross-ties, Considerable pains have been taken to get large sized ties, which, with the superior character of the new chair used, secures us a track equal to the best in the country. A great saving in the cost of repairs to machinery has been effected by the improved condition of our track. Our second track has been used as sidings or turnouts only. By laying $1\frac{1}{4}$ miles of track we will connect the sidings between Catasauqua and Laury's, giving us 7 miles of second track at a very desirable point for passing trains. This and the completion of the grading and laying the second track from Mauch Chunk to Parryville will add much to the capacity of our road and should be done as early as possible. The iron bridge erected at Easton proves to be a very permanent structure and is looked upon with favor by all who have examined it. A year's use has tended to strengthen my confidence in it. The bridge across the Saucon at Freemansburg (2 spans of 65 feet each), should be rebuilt during the coming summer. The bridge across the Little Lehigh at Allentown (2 spans of 130 feet each), is being replaced by an iron structure similar in principle and manner of construction to that at Easton. The bridge at Slatington, 106 feet span, that across Lizzard Creek, 86 feet span, and 4 spans of 82 feet each at Mauch Chunk, should be rebuilt this year. A new water tank and house of very substantial character have been built at Bethlehem, also new tanks at Whitehall and Parryville. A commodious and handsome brick station house for passengers has been built at Allentown. It is quite an ornament to the town and gives very general satisfaction to the citizens as well as the travelling public. A brick station for passengers and freight is nearly completed at Catasauqua. Plans have been prepared for passenger and freight house at Slatington, where it is much needed. The station house at Mauch Chunk has been enlarged and moved back far enough from the main track to admit of the laying an independent track upon which the freight and passenger cars may receive and discharge their cargoes without interrupting business upon the main line. The station house at Easton is the source of much anxiety on account of the combustible materials of which it is built, and the certainty of the destruction of it and the trestling in the event of its taking fire. It should be replaced with a stone structure and I am now having plans prepared for the same.

A frame building, 165 by 32 feet, has been erected at Mauch Chunk for housing our passenger cars. A very excellent iron turntable, 50 feet in diameter has been put in at Mauch Chunk. It was built by F. C. Lowthrop of Trenton, and is equal, if not superior to any I have seen, though costing $230 less than tables of that size usually do.

Our repair shops at South Easton are about completed and will compare favorably with any establishment of the kind in the country. They are built of stone, and consist of machine shop, 150 by 60 feet, boiler and blacksmith shop, 150 by 40 feet, car shop, 128 by 36 feet, two stories high, and engine house 40 by 30 feet. Arrangements have been made for having a full supply of water on hand at all times so as to be prepared in case of fire. When the reservoir is completed there will be sufficient head to force the water over our highest buildings. The equipment of the road has been increased by the addition of two first class freight engines built by Wm. Mason. 78 eight wheel iron truck coal cars, 2 first class baggage cars, 15 platform cars and 10 hand and gravel cars, all of which were built at our own shops, except 30 of the coal cars. We have lost one locomotive by explosion so that our equipment at present consists of 20 locomotives of all classes, 509 four wheel and 485 eight wheel coal cars, 34 eight wheel platform cars, 8 passenger cars, 4 baggage cars and 47 gravel and hand cars. The timber is on hand and all the iron work completed for building 51 eight wheeled coal cars.

The business from the Quakake and Eastern Pennsylvania Railroads shows a handsome increase and will no doubt continue to improve. From the former we have received about $14,800, and from the latter about $25,000. The Catasauqua and Fogelsville and Ironton Railroads each contribute to swell our business, and will, as the iron interests of our valley increase, extend their influence and add more largely to our income. A permanent location of the Penn Haven and White Haven Railroad has been made during the past summer. Examinations made demonstrate the fact that a good road can be built to connect the Lehigh and Susquehanna Railroad and Beaver Meadow Railroad, at a moderate cost, with maximum grades in the direction of the trade of 37 feet per mile, and no curve of less than 500 feet radius will be required. Great interest is felt in this enterprise by the coal operators in Wyoming Valley, and its completion will bring our road into the most direct and best route between Wyoming Valley and the cities of Philadelphia and New York. Two routes have been examined for connecting the great Mahanoy coal field with our road, thence to Trenton and New York by the Belvidere Delaware and Central Railroads. The first by way of Mahoning Valley to Tamauqua thence by Little Schuylkill and East Mahanoy Railroad, requiring 17 miles of new road, at a cost of say, $600,000. The second is by way of Beaver Meadow and Quakake Railroads, thence into the eastern end of Mahanoy Valley, requiring four or five miles of new road, at a cost of say, $75,000. The first named route will give us a good connection with the Schuylkill Valley and with the Sunbury and Erie via East Mahanoy and Mt. Carmel Railroads to Sunbury. The completion of the several links spoken of forming the connection, between the rich valleys of the Schuylkill and Susquehanna, and the cities of Philadelphia and New York, will have the effect of placing the Lehigh Valley Railroad foremost in the great carrying lines of the country.

Our local coal trade has increased handsomely during the year just passed, and an early adjustment of the political and financial difficulties of the country will enable me at the close of another year to record a still greater increase. There are now four first class blast furnaces and two rolling mill in the course of erection, which will consume about 100,000 tons of coal annually, all of which, together with portions of the ore, limestone, &c., and the product of the furnaces, may be secured to our road.

The completion of the bridge over the river connecting the Carbon Iron Works with our road, has resulted in securing to us a large share of their business. A third passenger train was put upon the road about the first of June, in order to make satisfactory connections with other roads. The result has been to decrease slightly our receipts per mile run, though it has given excellent facilities to the travelling public, and affords very general satisfaction.

By reference to the annexed tables you will see that the mileage of our engines has increased 88,191 miles, with the addition of but one engine to last year's number. This indicates a much heavier service for each engine; yet from the improved condition of our track and the superior character of our engines of recent purchase, our expenses for repairs of locomotives has been reduced 2 cents per mile run.

My acknowledgments are due to our officers and employees generally, for the faithful and diligent discharge of their duties, and especially so to Mr. Cox, who performed the duties of Superintendent during my absence of nearly five months.

Very respectfully yours,
ROBT. H. SAYRE,
Superintendent and Engineer.

LEHIGH VALLEY RAILROAD,
Office of Superintendent and Engineer.

BETHLEHEM, Nov. 30th, 1861.

J. G. FELL, Esq.,
President Lehigh Valley Railroad Co.

DEAR SIR:
The following report of the business of the Lehigh Valley Railroad for the fiscal year ending November 30, 1861, is respectfully submitted. The total amount of coal transported over the road was 743,672 tons, and was distributed as follows:

	1861.	1860.
To the Belvidere Delaware Railroad..	146,622	146,931 tons
" " Central Railroad of N. J.....	260,393	271,262 "
" " North Penna. Railroad......	98,389	91,327 "
" " East " "	10,622	11,030 "
" " Catasauqua & Fogelsville....	4,290	4,875 "
" " Ironton Railroad	1,141	463 "
" " Morris Canal	1,271	997 "
Delivered on line of road..........	220,944	203,757 "
	743,672	730,642 tons

Equal to 616,419 tons transported over the whole length of the road, or 28,355,279 tons transported one mile.

During the same period there were transported 181,086 passengers, equal to 57,161 over the whole length of the road, or one passenger transported 2,629,410 miles.

The pig iron and merchandise freight show a decrease. The iron ore, limestone, live stock and some other items show a satisfactory increase. The total freight tonnage, independent of coal, amounts to about 275,000 tons.

The following is a statement of the ordinary receipts and expenditures:

RECEIPTS.

From Coal Transportation.................	$499,877	92
" Passenger Express and Mail............	82,117	93
" Freight	97,495	45
	$679,491	30

EXPENDITURES.

For Coal Transportation........	$230,705	69		
" Passenger Express and Mail.	43,152	48		
" Freight ....,	47,479	48	321,337	65
			$358,153	65

Compared with last year the receipts from coal show a decrease of $14,652.48; from passengers an increase of $3,582.14; from freight an increase of $10,655.05; total gross receipts show a decrease of $417.29; total net receipts an increase of $16,164.99. The decrease in coal receipts is due to lower rates prevailing most of the season, and to a larger portion of the tonnage being used on the line of the road, and therefore transported shorter distances. The increase in passenger receipts is due to the transportation of troops. The increase in freight receipts is principally due to the live stock trade, which is $6,586.53 in excess of last year. The number of miles run by coal and freight trains was 203,060, and receipts per mile run $2.94. The number of miles run by passenger trains was 97,760, and receipts per mile run 84 cents. Total mileage of all the trains, including construction and drilling engines, was 339,840 miles. Receipts from all sources per mile run $2.00. Included in the ordinary expenses as above stated are the following items:

Railroad Iron	$36,891	09
Cross-ties, Chairs and Spikes.................	25,147	50
Iron Bridge at Allentown....................	21,528	26
Embankment and wall at Easton...............	3,106	81
Iron Turntable at South Easton...............	1,670	98

Arch over canal feeder at Mauch Chunk..........	1,611	40
River Bridge at Mauch Chunk (new)............	7,091	62
New Bridges across Mahoning and Fell's Creeks and repairs to other bridges...................	5,208	57

There have been charged to construction the following sums:

Engine house and machinery at Mauch Chunk....	$3,439	75
Water tank and fixtures......................	401	14
Mauch Chunk and Allentown station houses......	841	07
Scales at Mauch Chunk......................	355	87
Land at Parryville..........................	500	00
Passenger and freight house at Catasauqua.......	1,805	49
Water tanks at Bethlehem....................	392	21
Shops and machinery at South Easton...........	8,061	09
Reservoir at South Easton....................	2,076	47
House for master of machinery................	3,089	18
Second track and sidings.....................	16,852	83
Cross-ties, chairs and spikes..................	1,856	90
Car house, &c.............................	341	11
	$40,013	11

There have been 2.1 miles of second track laid and 1.7 miles of second track and sidings relaid with new iron. There are now in use 17.7 miles of second track and 6.3 miles of sidings. 2.9 miles of second track have been graded and there are now 11.4 miles ready for the ballast and track. The detached pieces of second track between Catasauqua and Laury's heretofore used as sidings have been connected and used as second track since June last. This has materially increased the capacity of the road and has been of much service in enabling trains to pass without the vexatious delays heretofore encountered. At no time since the opening of the road has the heavy business been done with so much regularity. The permanent way has been very much improved during the year. At Easton 750 feet of trestling has been removed and a double track embankment with heavy wall between the branches connecting the Belvidere Delaware and Central Railroads substituted. 168 feet more of trestling have been rebuilt. A bridge of 36 feet span over the public road near Freemansburg has been rebuilt. One of 32 feet span over the railroad at Catasauqua, and one of 36 feet span over the railroad at Lehighton have been rebuilt. Abutments have been built at Rockdale and Slatington bridges, shortening the spans of each 24 feet, and making them of uniform length with the spans at Mauch Chunk. Two piers have been put in at Lizzard Creek preparatory to replacing the wooden structure with one of stone, 3 arches—each 20 feet span. The trestling over the canal feeder at Mauch Chunk has been removed and a stone arch, $8\frac{1}{2}$ feet span, 183 feet long, substituted. At Allentown there have been two spans (of 125 feet each) of double track iron bridge erected. It is similar in principle to that built at Easton two years since. They are very firm permanent structures, and I hope all the bridges to be rebuilt hereafter will be of the same character. At Laury's one span of 50 feet double track, at Lehighton one span of 62 feet double track, and at Mauch Chunk 4 spans (each 82 feet) double track have been rebuilt. These structures are of wood, but are of a substantial character, and will, I think, be safe for eight or ten years. Between Whitehall and Coplay stations three double track bridges have been renewed, one of 20 feet span, one of 24 and one of 45 feet.

The bridge across the Delaware canal needs some repairs and the material has been ordered for it. The balance of the river bridge is in good order, except the branch bridge connecting with the Belvidere Delaware Railroad. The materials for the repair of this are now on hand. The bridge across the canal at Mauch Chunk, those at Slatington, Rockdale, and Shimersville must be renewed next year. I would also recommend the renewal of at least one span per annum of river bridge at Easton, until the whole has been replaced by a permanent iron structure. The track has been kept in excellent repair and no accident whatever has occurred from defects in it. Eight miles have been ballasted and there are now 48 miles of track ballasted with broken stone or cinder. 900 tons of new iron, together with 45,877 cross-ties, 487 kegs of spikes and 4,453 chairs have been used in repairs. The Fisher & Norris chair, which was adopted about three years since, continues to give entire satisfaction. It is, I think, without doubt the best chair that can be had for the price. What is now particularly wanted to give us a first class track and reduce the annual expense of its repairs is a better quality of iron. None that we have ever used, except that purchased from the Phoenix Iron Works, when the track was first laid, has proved really good. A subsequent purchase from the same establishment was found to be no better than that used from other works. If an advance of ten dollars upon the price usually paid will secure iron of first quality, I am well satisfied that no investment that can be made will yield so large and satisfactory a return. A reservoir, 120 by 100 feet square and 8 feet deep, of a capacity of 600,000 gallons, has been completed on the hill in the rear of our shops at South Easton. The water is pumped into it from the canal by the shop power. The bottom of it is some 30 feet higher than the tops of our buildings. More attachments have been placed in the pipe leading from it, so that the entire premises may be flooded in case of fire. A new water tank was built about one mile below Slatington and one at Mauch Chunk. A brick building, 26 by 42 was erected at Mauch Chunk, in which was placed a 15-horse power engine. It is used for pumping water, sawing wood, driving the machinery in the repair shop, and furnishes blast for the blacksmith's fires. An addition 20 by 50 was built to the repair shop, in which has been placed a planing machine and circular saw.

The wooden turntable at South Easton having become much decayed, it has been replaced by one of Lowthrop's patent cast-iron tables, 55 feet in diameter, similar to the one put in at Mauch Chunk last year, which continues to work admirably. The passenger and freight house at Catasauqua was completed early in the spring. New station houses are very much needed at Bethlehem and Slatington.

At the date of my last report we had just occupied our new shops at South Easton. A year's use has shown their utility and convenience. The superior character of the work done and great reduction in the cost of repairs is excellent evidence of the value of having good shops and machinery. To complete our establishment at that point there should be added a foundry, a car house for sheltering the passenger cars and a building for piling the lumber in, that is used in building and repairing cars. The repair shop at Mauch Chunk is a frame building erected upon ground belonging to the Lehigh Coal and Navigation Company, for which we pay a ground rent of $100 per annum. It is liable to be burned, both from the sparks from locomotives and from its close proximity to a boat yard, which has twice been on fire since we occupied the shop. These facts in connection with that of the insufficiency of room in that vicinity for sidings upon which to make up the coal trains, induces me to recommend to your consideration the propriety of the Company's purchasing some 15 acres of the flat situated about three-quarters of a mile below the bridge, upon which to erect suitable repair shops and the necessary sidings for our coal business. We now use the second track from Mauch Chunk to the location spoken of for stand room for loaded cars. When our business requires the second track to run upon we will be unable to make up trains for the present business without making additional sidings, which, in my opinion, will cost more than to purchase the property named. The road equipment has been kept in first rate order and has been increased by the building of 30 eight wheel iron-truck coal cars. It now consists of 20 locomotives, 509 four wheel and 515 eight wheel coal cars, 34 eight wheel platform cars, 8 passenger and 4 baggage cars and 47 gravel and hand cars. Two new freight engines have been ordered from the establishment of Wm. Mason, to be similar in all respects to four now in use upon the road from the same maker.

The great economy of having the different class engines employed of uniform pattern is so evident that I would much prefer it (even if they were inferior in some particulars) to having a dozen different patterns with all the so-called improvements. Of 20 locomotives now in use, 4 are exactly alike, and consequently require but a single duplicate piece of any part liable to wear out or break to be kept on hand. The remaining 16 engines are of 12 different patterns, requiring 12 duplicate pieces or parts to be kept on hand. By referring to the annexed table of engine statistics you will perceive that the average mileage of the 4 Mason engines was 23,235 miles, at a cost of repairs of 4.78 cents per mile, while the average mileage of 6 other engines performing the same kind of service, was 12,651 miles, at a cost of 11.66 cents per mile. A part of this great difference is due to the fact that the first-named engines have not been so long in service, and are of superior workmanship, but much of it is in consequence of the uniformity of pattern. The passenger and freight traffic to and from the Central Railroad and East Pennsylvania Railroad exhibits a very decided increase.

The revenue accruing to our road from passengers and freight (other than coal) to and from the connecting roads is as follows:

Central Railroad of New Jersey	$78,629 18
East Pennsylvania Railroad	43,400 01
North Pennsylvania Railroad	27,871 76
Catawissa Railroad	14,855 46

Our business relations with the several connecting roads has been harmonious and pleasant. A location has been made for the extension of the Quakake Railroad into the Mahanoy and Shenandoah coal basins. It is proposed to build ten miles from the junction, six of which will be over coal. It can be completed at a cost of say, $150,000. Measures are being taken that will secure the building of it at an early day. It will, I think, add largely to our coal tonnage. A charter has been secured and location made for a railroad from Mauch Chunk to the Mahanoy tunnel and North Mahanoy basin via Nesquehoning Valley. It is intended to be built by parties owning the canal between Mauch Chunk and tidewater, but a connection with our road at Mauch Chunk will secure to it the tonnage during the winter season at least.

The coal from Mahanoy Valley via the tunnel destined for New York water, can only be secured during the entire season, by our building the Mahoning branch. This, I believe, the true interests of the Company demand, and should be done speedily. Nothing has been done upon the Penn Haven and White Haven Railroad since the date of my last report. The disturbed state of the political and financial affairs of the country rendering it imprudent to attempt the further prosecution of the enterprise for the present. It is, however, a very important connection, and its completion at as early a day as circumstances will admit of, very desirable, as it will undoubtedly be a paying improvement and add largely to the receipts of our road.

In conclusion, permit me to say, that it is gratifying to again bear testimony to the faithfulness and diligence of the heads of the various departments of transportation and repairs, and to the employees generally.

Very respectfully yours,
ROBT. H. SAYRE,
Superintendent and Engineer.

[*Reprint March 15, 1899.*]

SEVENTH

ANNUAL REPORT

OF THE

BOARD OF MANAGERS

OF THE

LEHIGH VALLEY RAIL-ROAD COMPANY.

JANUARY 12, 1863.

MAUCH CHUNK:
TOLAN & HIBBS, PRINTERS.
1863.

[*Reprint March 15, 1899.*]

SEVENTH

ANNUAL REPORT

OF THE

BOARD OF MANAGERS

OF THE

LEHIGH VALLEY RAIL-ROAD COMPANY.

JANUARY 12, 1863.

MAUCH CHUNK:
TOLAN & HIBBS, PRINTERS.
1863.

OFFICERS AND MANAGERS

OF THE

LEHIGH VALLEY RAIL ROAD COMPANY,

FOR 1863.

PRESIDENT,
ASA PACKER.

MANAGERS,

R. F. STOCKTON,	JOHN TAYLOR JOHNSTON,
E. A. PACKER,	J. G. FELL,
JOHN N. HUTCHINSON,	W. H. GATZMER,
JOSIAH O. STEARNS.	ASHBEL WELCH,
ROBERT A. PACKER,	JOHN KNECHT,
EDWARD H. TROTTER,	DAVID THOMAS.

SECRETARY AND TREASURER,
WM. H. ELY.

ENGINEER AND SUPERINTENDENT,
ROBERT H. SAYRE.

SEVENTH ANNUAL REPORT

OF THE

BOARD OF MANAGERS

OF THE

Lehigh Valley Rail-road Company.

The Managers of the Lehigh Valley Rail-Road Company present to the Stockholders the following Report, for the year ending November 29th, 1862.

The amount of Coal transported over the road was 882,574 Tons, and was distributed as follows:

	1862.	1861.
To the Central Rail Road of New Jersey..	306,824 Tons.	260,393 Tons.
" Belvidere Delaware Rail Road.....	125.503 "	146,622 "
" North Pennsylvania Rail Road....	103,947 "	98,389 "
" Morris Canal.....................	43,296 "	1,271 "
" Delaware Canal..................	29,605 "	
" East Pennsylvania Rail Road......	6,667 "	10,622 "
" Catasauqua and Fogelsville R. R..	2,257 "	4,290 "
" Ironton Rail Road...............	1,214 "	1,141 "
Delivered on line of the Road............	263,261 "	220,944 "
Total.........	882,574 "	743,672 "

Equal to 747,930 tons transported over the whole length of the road.

During the same period there were transported 193,246 passengers, equal to 61,152 over the whole length of the road.

The miscellaneous freight, which includes Pig Iron, Lime Stone, Lumber, Live Stock, Merchandise, &c., show a very decided and satisfactory increase, and amounts to about 420,000 tons.

The following is a statement of the ordinary receipts and expenditures :

RECEIPTS.

From Coal Transportation	$630,624	90
" Passengers, Express and Mail Transportation	89,470	27
" Freight Transportation	135,959	36
	$856,054	53

EXPENDITURES.

For Coal Transportation	$295,724	22		
" Passenger, Express and Mail Transp'n	48,192	76		
" Freight Transportation	63,635	84	$407,552	82
Balance, nett earnings			$448,501	71
Balance to credit of profit and loss acc't., Nov. 30, 1861			176,324	99
			$624,826	70

Against which has been charged :

Dividend paid May 1, 1862, four per cent on Capital Stock, $2,297,250.00	$91,890	00		
Dividend paid Nov. 1, 1862, four per cent on Capital Stock, $2,297,250.00	91,890	00		
Six per cent on $1,465,000 Bonds	87,900	00		
Taxes	1,533	50	$273,213	50
Leaving a balance of profits Nov. 29, 1862, of			$351,613	20

Against which is to be charged as a renewal fund, depreciation in rolling stock, and unfinished repairs of damages by freshet, &c.

Compared with last year, the

Receipts from Coal show an increase of.................. $130,746 98
    "   " Passengers   " 7,352 31
    "   " Freight   " 38,463 91
Increase in Receipts.................... $176,563 20, or 25.9 per cent.
Increase in Expenses.................... 86,415 17, or 26.8 per cent.
Increase in Nett Receipts................ 90,148 03, or 25.1 per cent.

Included in the ordinary expenses, as above stated, are the following items:

Damages by high water (as far as paid)........$55,392 66
Rail Road Iron............................... 65,993 54
Cross-ties, Chairs and Spikes................. 13,174 06
New Bridges.... .... 8,719 79
Sundry Claims and Damages by fire........... 1,990 47
                                                         $145,270 52

During the year there has been charged:

To Construction................................ ....$34,104 20
To Car Account,... 66,040 05
To Real Estate... 2,715 68
To Locomotives...................................... ..... 68,386 65

The condensed balance sheet, herewith submitted, shows the financial condition of the Company.

There was laid during the year 3.42 miles of second track, and 1.34 miles of sidings. A portion of this was carried away by the freshet, but most of it has been relaid, and there is now in use 20.1 miles of second track, and 7.5 miles of sidings. There is 9.8 miles of second track graded and ready for the track.

On the night of the 4th, and morning of the 5th, of June, there occurred the most destructive freshet ever known in the Lehigh Valley. Our road suffered very considerable injuries, and coal shipments were suspended until the 8th of July.

The superstructure and masonry of the bridges across the canal and river near Mauch Chunk, and the superstructure of the Mahoning Creek Bridge were swept away; the bridge across the public road near Hockendauqua was removed from its foundation; the bridge across the street below Allentown station was displaced; the iron bridge across the Little Lehigh was raised up by the accumulation of drift-wood under it, and some of the parts displaced.

One of the piers of the bridge over the Delaware was seriously injured. Three and one-quarter miles of the embankment of main track were very much washed, and a large portion of it entirely gone; about two miles more of it so injured as to need repairs to make it safe for business.

Over five miles of the main-track was moved from its bed; some of it turned upside down and covered with gravel; other portions of it carried into the river, the iron bent and broken, and some of it entirely lost. 4.3 miles of second-track embankment was washed away, and nearly one and a half miles of track was removed from its bed, and portions of it lost.

The water had so far receded on the morning of the 6th as to enable us to commence repairs, which were prosecuted with vigor.

Our passenger trains were run from Easton to Allentown on the evening of the 7th; to Laury's on the morning of the 10th; to Slatington on the morning of the 12th;

to the bridge below Mauch Chunk on the evening of the 18th ; and to Mauch Chunk station on the evening of July 3d.

The repairs of the Beaver Meadow Road not being finished, the coal business was not resumed until the 8th, between which time and November 29th, there were 500,647 tons of coal transported over the road. .

The masonry for the canal and river bridge is nearly completed, and an iron superstructure is in course of construction.

A stone arch of eight and a half feet span over Beaver Run, and a stone viaduct of three spans of twenty-two feet each, have been built over Lizzard Creek ; a double track timber bridge, of sixty-two feet span, for the Mahoning Creek, is framed and ready to be put up.

At Slatington a new passenger and freight house, and a double track wooden bridge of eighty-two feet span are nearly completed.

Most of the work has been done upon two spans, of sixty two feet each, of iron bridge, to replace the wooden structure at Freemansburg ; 324 feet lineal of double track trestling, at Easton Depot, has been renewed.

New arches have been put upon the span of bridge over the Delaware canal, and the pier which was injured thoroughly repaired.

The track is now in good order, though not quite so permanent and smooth as it was previous to the freshet.

Efforts were made to increase our motive power and cars to meet the requirements of the trade, but were not entirely successful. 72,254 tons of coal from the Lehigh region passed over the Reading Rail-road, via Quakake, in consequence of our incapacity to meet the sudden demand made upon us in consequence of the destruction of the canal.

Six first-class freight and two passenger engines were put on the road during the year, and two more first-class freight engines have been ordered from Wm. Mason & Co., to be delivered in April next.

There have been built at our shops—

    110 eight wheel iron truck Coal cars.
    12 " " " Flat cars.
    6 four " " Coal cars.
    and 16 eight " " Coal cars purchased.

There were about fifteen coal cars lost by the freshet, and some twenty more badly damaged.

The iron works on the line of our road are prospering, and now bid fair to give us a large increase of tonnage next year.

The work of extending the Quakake Rail-road into the Mahanoy coal basin, has progressed favorably, and it is expected to open the Road as far as Mahanoy City in the Spring, when we may expect an addition to our coal tonnage from that region.

The Penn Haven and White Haven Rail-road was put under contract last July, and has been pushed as vigorously as the scarcity of labor would admit. Fully one-fourth of the work is now done, and it is expected to open the line for business, through to Wyoming Valley, next fall.

It is expected that the Schuylkill Haven and Lehigh River Rail-road will be completed within the year 1863. This, with the great desire of the Schuylkill coal operators to reach New York waters by a continuous rail route throughout the year, will without doubt, induce a large coal tonnage.

In view of these improvements the double tracking of our road becomes a necessity, and we have taken such measures as will secure its completion within the next year.

It remains for us to say that the Company are much indebted to their various officers for the faithful and diligent discharge of their duties.

By order of the Board.

ASA PACKER, President.

Mauch Chunk, Pa.,
January 12, 1863.

CONDENSED BALANCE SHEET—NOVEMBER 29th, 1862.

DR.		CR.	
Capital Stock	$2,297,250 00	Rail-road	$2,958,077 35
Bonds	1,465,000 00	Locomotives	250,890 42
Balance to the credit of interest and transportation accounts	448,501 71	Rail-road Cars	425,207 74
		Passenger Cars	12,692 00
Coupons overdue	5,421 30	Construction	422,543 70
Dividends overdue	11,346 00	Tamaqua Extension	1,189 80
Scrip Stock	55,985 00	Real Estate	12,468 18
Debts due by the Company	40,381 58	Machine Shop	16,752 31
		Telegraph Line	3,735 86
		Profit and Loss Account	96,888 51
		Quakake Rail-road	11,888 29
		Cash	42,827 53
		Penn Haven and White Haven R. R. Co.	24,829 60
		Penn Haven and White Haven R.R. Stock	150 00
		Debts due the Company	43,744 39
	$4,323,885 59		$4,323,885 59

WM. H. ELY, *Treasurer*

LEHIGH VALLEY RAILROAD,
Office of Superintendent and Engineer.

BETHLEHEM, Nov. 30, 1862.

ASA PACKER, Esq.,
President Lehigh Valley Railroad Company.

DEAR SIR:

The following report of the business of the Lehigh Valley Railroad for the fiscal year ending November 30, 1862, is respectfully submitted.

The total amount of coal transported over the road was 882,547 tons, and was distributed as follows:

		1862.	1861.
Delivered on the line of the road		263,261	220,944 tons
"	Ironton Railroad	1,214	1,141 "
"	Cat. & Fogelsville R. R.	2,257	4,290 "
"	East Penna. Railroad	6,667	10,622 "
"	North Penna. Railroad	103,947	98,389 "
"	Delaware Canal	29,605	—
"	Belvidere Delaware R. R.	125,503	146,622 "
"	Morris Canal	43,296	1,271 "
"	Central R. R. of N. J.	306,824	260,393 "
		882,574	743,672 tons

Equal to 747,930 tons transported over the whole length of road or 34,404,795 tons transported one mile. During the same period there were transported 193,246 passengers, equal to 61,152 over the whole length of road, or 2,812,980 passengers transported one mile. The miscellaneous freight, which includes pig iron, iron ore, limestone, lumber, live stock, merchandise, &c., &c., shows a very decided and satisfactory increase and amounts to about 420,000 tons. Much of this tonnage is moved but a short distance, and on part of it we receive tolls only.

The following is a statment of the receipts and expenditures:

RECEIPTS.

From Coal Transportation...................	$630,624 90
" Passenger, Express and Mail...........	89,470 27
" Freight	135,959 36
	$856,054 53

EXPENDITURES.

For Coal Transportation........	$295,724 22	
" Passenger, Express and Mail..	48,192 76	
" Freight	63,635 84	407,552 82
		$448,501 71

Compared with last year the receipts from coal show an increase of................................ $130,746 98
From passengers an increase of.............. 7,352 31
From freight an increase of................. 38,463 91

Increase in receipts............. $176,563.20 or 25.9 per cent.
"   " expenses .... 86,415.17 or 26.8   "
"   " net receipts........ 90,148.03 or 25.1   "

The mileage of trains and earnings per mile run were as follows:

	1862.		1861.	
	Miles.	Earnings.	Miles.	Earnings.
Coal and freight trains.......	229,880	3.33\frac{4}{10}$	203,060	$2.94
Passenger trains.............	97,450	.91$\frac{8}{10}$	97,760	.84
Drilling & construction trains.	43,390		39,020	
	370,720	2.30\frac{8}{10}$	339,840	$2.00

Included in the ordinary expenses as above stated are the following items:

Damages by high water....................	$55,392 66
Railroad iron (400 tons on hand).............	65,993 54
Cross-ties, chairs and spikes................	13,174 06
New bridges	8,719 79
Damages to persons and property............	1,990 47

There has been charged to construction as follows:

New track	$30,827	68
Shops at Mauch Chunk and South Easton	1,269	29
Tool houses, &c.	199	70
Reservoir	568	49
Slatington depôt and Gap water tank	439	04
Land at Glendon	800	00
	$34,104	20

There were laid during the year 3.42 miles of second track and 1.34 miles of sidings, a portion of this was carried away by the freshet, but most of it has been relaid, and there are now in use 20.1 miles of second track and 7.5 miles of sidings. There are 9.8 miles of second track graded and ready for the track. On the night of the 4th and the morning of the 5th of June there occurred the most destructive freshet ever known in the Lehigh Valley. Our road suffered very considerable injuries, and coal shipments were suspended until the 8th of July. The superstructure and masonry of the bridges across the canal and river near Mauch Chunk and the superstructure of the Mahoning Creek bridge were swept away. The bridge across the public road near Hokendauqua was removed from its foundation, the bridge across the street below Allentown station was displaced, the iron bridge across the Little Lehigh was raised up by the accumulation of drift wood under it and some of the parts displaced. One of the piers of the bridge over the Delaware was seriously injured. 3¼ miles of the embankment of main track were very much washed and a large portion of it entirely gone, about 2 miles more of it so injured as to need repairs to make it safe for business. Over 5 miles of the main track were moved from its bed; some of it was turned upside down and covered with gravel, other portions of it carried into the river, the iron bent and broken, and some of it entirely lost. 4.3 miles of second track embankment were washed away, and nearly 1½ miles of track were removed from its bed and portions of it lost. The water had so far receded in the morning of the 6th as to enable us to commence repairs, which were prosecuted with vigor. Our passenger trains were run from Easton to Allentown on the evening of the 7th, to Laury's on the morning of the 10th, to Slatington on the morning of the 12th. The track was laid through to south end of the bridge near Mauch Chunk and a portion of the timber for the trestle work delivered there on the evening of the 18th. A rise of between 5 and 6 feet in the river retarded the progress of the work, but the trestling was finally completed and the passenger trains run over the evening of July 3rd. The repairs of the Beaver Meadow road not being finished the coal business was not resumed until the 8th, between which time and November 30th, there were 500,-647 tons of coal transported over the road. On the afternoon of Saturday, October 4th, the iron bridge which was in the course of erection across the canal by the contractors gave way under a coal train, precipitating the bridge and nineteen coal cars into the canal. The wreck was removed so as to allow the passage of boats by Monday evening, and the trestling completed for the passage of trains on Wednesday noon. Two men who were at work under the bridge when it fell were killed. The masonry for the canal and river bridge is nearly completed, and an iron superstructure is in course of construction. A stone arch of $8\frac{1}{2}$ feet span over Beaver Run and a stone viaduct of three spans of 22 feet each has been built over Lizzard Creek. A double track timber bridge of 62 feet span for Mahoning Creek is framed and ready to be put up. A new water tank of a capacity of 44,000 gallons has been built at the Gap. At Slatington a new passenger and freight house and a double track wooden bridge of 82 feet span are nearly completed. Most of the work has been done upon two spans of 62 feet each of iron bridge to replace the wooden structure at Freemansburg. 324 feet, lineal, of double track trestling at Easton depôt have been renewed. New arches have been put upon the span of bridge over the Delaware Canal, and the pier which was injured, thoroughly repaired. Nearly a mile of sidings have been put in at Glendon for stand room.

22,112 cross-ties, 880 tons of iron, 3,408 chairs and 341 kegs of spikes have been used in repairs, and 11,272 cross-ties, 382 tons of iron, 746 new chairs and 182 kegs of spikes have been used in construction. The track is now in good order, though not quite so permanent and smooth as it was previous to the freshet. Much of the ballast was washed out and the new banks continue to settle. Efforts were made to increase our motive power and cars to meet the requirements of the trade, but were not entirely successful. About 100,000 tons of coal from the Lehigh region passed over the Reading Railroad via Quakake in consequence of our incapacity to meet the sudden demand made upon us in consequence of the destruction of the canal. Two first class freight engines were received from Mason* and placed upon the road early in the year. Another from Baldwin† in August, and two from Mason and one from Baldwin in the latter part of November. Also a passenger engine from Baldwin in the early part of November.

In May, one of our largest engines, Norris,‡ builder, exploded, killing the engineer and fireman. The remaining engine of same class was taken to the shop and a new boiler built for it. It has not yet been put in use. There have been built at our shops 110 eight wheel iron-truck coal cars. 12 eight wheel iron-truck flat cars and 6 four wheel coal cars, and 16 eight wheel iron-truck coal cars purchased. There were about 15 coal cars lost by the freshet and some 20 more badly damaged. Two freight engines have been ordered from Mason to be delivered in April next. I would recommend the order being increased to six, to be delivered during the summer and fall.

2,000 coal cars and 200 flat cars will be wanted next year to meet the wants of the coal and lumber trade. Our present facilities will not enable us to build over 200 eight wheel cars.

Next in importance to rolling stock is a want of ground for tracks upon which to make up trains for the connecting roads. We have been notified by the Central Railroad Company that we must deliver their loaded cars at Phillipsburg and furnish track room at South Easton for empty cars coming from their road. This is not practicable under the present system of doing our business. We receive the cars at Mauch Chunk for three connecting roads and two canals, mixed up in every conceivable shape. There are not sufficient facilities there to assort them

---

* Locomotive Builder, Taunton, Mass.
† Locomotive Builder, Philadelphia, Pa.
‡ Locomotive Builder, Philadelphia, Pa.

properly, and it has therefore to a great extent to be done at South Easton. This occupies all the track room we can possibly get there, leaving no place for empty cars. During the past season it has required two drilling engines and crews to drill trains. Much of this expense might be avoided by drilling the cars at Mauch Chunk or Penn Haven, where it could be done by gravity. A want of room at Penn Haven would seem to make it necessary to be done at or near Mauch Chunk, where ground will have to be purchased and the necessary tracks put in. Heretofore we have borne the whole of this expense, but I would suggest that in the future all parties in interest should participate. The difficulties and annoyances attending the various ownership of cars is constantly increasing. I would therefore earnestly recommend that some plan should be devised and adopted to remedy the evils. The true interests of all the transportation Companies demand it, and I feel confident that a serious consideration of the matter will satisfy you of its importance and induce prompt action upon the subject. The iron works on the line of our road are prospering and now bid fair to give us a large increase of tonnage next year. The Thomas Iron Company expect to blow in one of their new stacks during the winter. I understand the Messrs. Thomas design erecting a rolling mill at Catasauqua and Mr. Lewis is about building one at Allentown Furnace. The Allentown Rolling Mill has been in successful operation since May last. The Bethlehem Iron Company expect to make pig metal the first of the year, and rails in April next. The Glendon Iron Company have built a substantial bridge across the canal connecting their works with our road, all of which will add largely to our tonnage. The time is not remote when we will be required to transport a million tons of coal to supply the iron works on the line.

The revenue accruing to this road from passenger travel and miscellaneous freight to and from the connecting roads is as follows:

	1862.	1861.
Central Railroad of New Jersey	$98,192 60	$78,629 18
East Pennsylvania Railroad	52,746 34	43,400 01
North " "	36,626 81	27,871 76
Catawissa "	21,249 52	14,855 46

Since the date of my last report the work of extending the Quakake Railroad into the Mahanoy coal basin has progressed favorably, and it is expected to open the road as far as Mahanoy City in the spring, when we may expect an addition to our coal tonnage from that region.

The Penn Haven and White Haven Railroad was put under contract last July, and has been pushed as vigorously as the scarcity of labor will admit. There have been expended to this date for graduation and masonry $39,575, fully one-fourth of the work is now done, and it is expected to open the line for business through to Wyoming Valley early next fall. It is being graded for a single track with sufficient sidings for a business of say, 500,000 tons. The grades are in the direction of the trade, maximum 37 feet per mile, radius of shortest curve 520 feet. In addition to the coal tonnage to be derived from this connection there will be about 40 millions of feet of lumber, manufactured annually in the upper Lehigh region, all of which will pass over the Penn Haven and White Haven, and at least half of it over the Lehigh Valley Railroad. The distance between Wilkesbarre and Philadelphia via Catawissa and Reading Railroads is 188 miles. Via Delaware, Lackawanna and Western and Belvidere Delaware Railroads is 184 miles. Via Penn Haven and White Haven, Lehigh Valley and North Pennsylvania is 134 miles. This great difference in distance in favor of our line will without doubt give us the entire passenger and miscellaneous freight business between Wyoming Valley and Philadelphia.

Notices have been issued to receive proposals for the building of the Schuylkill Haven and Lehigh River Railroad, the work to be completed within the year 1863. I am informed that the work will be light, grades and curves easy, and cost low, all of which, together with the great desire of the Schuylkill coal operators to reach New York waters by a continuous rail route throughout the year, will, without doubt, induce a large coal tonnage. The road is designed to cross the Little Schuylkill at Ringgold, ten miles below Tamauqua, and to connect with the Lehigh Valley at or near the mouth of Lizzard Creek, about seven miles below Mauch Chunk. In view of these improvements the double tracking of our road becomes a necessity, and I have taken such measures as will secure its completion within the next year. The very short curve in our road at Mauch Chunk and the large amount of business to be done there makes it desirable that our facilities should be increased. It is proposed to do this by driving a double track tunnel through the mountain at that point. A survey and location has been made leaving our main line at the bridge and penetrating the mountain in a direct line with it, connecting with the Beaver Meadow Railroad about 1,800 feet above our present junction with it. The tunnel will be 2,400 feet long, the entire line 3,350 feet, with grade of 46.87 per mile. The line around the hill is 6,842 feet long, with grades varying from 10 to 33 feet per mile and curve of 320 feet radius. It is proposed to run the coal and through freight trains through the tunnel and the passenger and way freight around the hill.

My acknowledgments are due to the heads of the various departments of transportation and repairs and to the employees generally for their faithfulness and diligent attention to their duties. Also to Mr. Samuel Thomas for securing the iron bridge at Allentown, and to David Thomas, Jr., for replacing the bridge at Hokendauqua in its proper position after the freshet.

Very respectfully yours,
ROBT. H. SAYRE,
Superintendent and Engineer.

LEHIGH VALLEY RAILROAD,
Office of the Superintendent and Engineer.

BETHLEHEM, November 30, 1863.

ASA PACKER, Esq.,
President Lehigh Valley Railroad Company.

DEAR SIR:

The following report of the business of the Lehigh Valley Railroad for the fiscal year ending November 30, 1863, is respectfully submitted.

The total amount of coal transported over the road was 1,195,155 tons, and was distributed as follows:

	1863.	1862.
Delivered on the line of the road	396,504	264,475
" Catasauqua & Fogelsville R. R.	1,833	2,257
" East Pennsylvania "	9,526	6,667
" North " "	113,680	103,947
" Delaware Canal	13,894	29,605
" Belvidere Delaware Railroad	137,061	125,503
" Morris Canal	48,884	43,296
" Central Railroad of N. J.	473,773	306,824
Total	1,195,155	882,574

Equal to 1,009,910 tons transported over the whole length of the road, or 46,455,867 tons transported one mile.

During the same period there were transported 266,235½ passengers, equal to 78,183 over the whole length of road, or 3,596,418 transported one mile. The freight, other than coal, continues to increase rapidly and amounts to 447,848 tons.

The following is a statement of the receipts and expenditures:

	Receipts.	Expenditures.
From Coal Transportation	$1,075,545 65	$459,264 88
" Passenger Express & Mail	118,449 54	60,004 95
" Freight	176,080 61	69,829 61
	$1,370,075 80	$589,099 44

Net............ $780,976 36

Compared with last year the receipts from coal show an increase of $444,920.75 or 70.5 per cent.; from passengers an increase of $28,979.29 or 32.3 per cent.; from freight an increase of $40,121.25 or 29.5 per cent.
Increase in Receipts $514,021.27 or 60 per cent.
Increase in Expenses $181,546.77 or 44.5 per cent.
Increase in Net Receipts $332,474.50 or 76.3 per cent.

The mileage of trains and earnings per mile run were as follows:

	1863.		1862.	
	Miles Run.	Earnings per Mile.	Miles Run.	Earnings per Mile.
Coal and freight trains	292,280	4.08\frac{5}{10}$	229,880	3.33\frac{4}{10}$
Passenger trains	101,305	1.16$\frac{9}{10}$	97,450	.91$\frac{8}{10}$
Drilling, repair & construct'n trains	70,955		43,390	
	463,640	2.95\frac{5}{10}$	370,720	2.30\frac{4}{10}$

Included in the expenses as above stated are the following items:

Railroad iron, cross-ties, chairs and spikes	$66,493 21
Repairs and renewals of bridges	10,904 84
High water damages	56,522 98

There was charged to construction the following:

Graduation, masonry, &c.	$135,705 25
Railroad iron	75,099 80
Cross-ties, chairs, spikes and switches	28,681 82

Shops and engine house at South Easton and Burlington, grading of grounds, &c........	35,145	18
Depôts, store house, &c....................	5,294	88
Water tanks, &c...........................	1,123	37
Total..........................	$281,050	30
New coal and flat cars....................	·153,296	62
Locomotives	51,968	94
Real estate...............................	13,765	80
	$500,081	66

There were laid during the year 13.9 miles of second track and 4 miles of sidings, and there are now in use 34 miles of second track and 11.5 miles of sidings. The grading for the balance of the second track is complete with the exception of about 1.5 miles which will be ready for the track as early as it can be laid. There were used in repairs 13,725 cross-ties, 776 tons of iron, 2,387 chairs and 308 kegs of spikes; and in construction 49,465 cross-ties, 1,246 tons of iron, 6,414 chairs and 1,015 kegs of spikes.

The road has been much improved since the date of my last report and is in good order, with the exception of some defective iron, which is now being renewed, all iron to be used in repairs and second track will be 30 feet long, thereby reducing the number of joints 25 per cent. and materially improving the track. All the bridges upon the line have been renewed except those at Easton. An iron one is now being built at our shops to cross the public road at that station. Those across Mahoning Creek, Balliet's Creek and the Delaware River are the only timber bridges of any length upon the road; the first two are good, being new; the latter must be rebuilt soon, whether it shall be of timber or iron remains for the Directors to determine. Considerable difficulty is apprehended in the renewal of this bridge, in consequence of there being a track upon both the upper and lower chords, and of the necessity of keeping the channel clear in seasons of rafting. It is questionable whether it would not be better to lengthen the abutments and piers and build a new bridge beside the old one. The cost of the masonry would be partially overcome by the reduced cost of erecting the new structure without interference from the passing trains, the amount of tonnage and the number of trains crossing and re-crossing will, I think, render it necessary in a very few years to provide additional tracks across the river; if done now we would be prepared for a large increase of business in the future.

The only interruption to the business of the road during the past year occurred on Friday, January 16th, when, by reason of heavy rains, the river rose nine feet above low water. Large quantities of logs and other drift, together with a bridge that had been erected across the river above Mauch Chunk, were brought down against our trestling carrying away a number of the bents. The track was repaired and trains passed over on Thursday the 22nd. An iron bridge was built at Mauch Chunk connecting the railroad with the town, at the joint expense of this Company and the Lehigh Coal and Navigation Company. The double track iron bridge across the canal and river near Mauch Chunk, three spans of 115 feet each, and one of 142 feet, was finished early in the summer. It is a handsome and substantial structure and will, I trust, relieve us from any further detention or trouble at that point.

A double track timber bridge was erected across Mahoning Creek, replacing a temporary one built after the freshet of June, 1862. The bridge at Slatington, which was in course of construction last year, was finished early this season.

A double track timber bridge of 80 feet span, and two of 32 feet span each, were built at Rockdale. Two spans of 60 feet each of iron have been built across the Saucon Creek near Freemansburg, in addition to which there were a number of short timber bridges built on the second track. A 9 feet arch culvert was lengthened 10 feet and an $8\frac{1}{2}$ arch lengthened 62 feet to accommodate a change and improvement of line.

The flat at Burlington, containing over 47 acres, has been purchased, upon which it is proposed to erect all the buildings, shops, tracks, &c., necessary for our rapidly increasing business. Trains will be made up at that point for the various connecting roads, thus avoiding much of the drilling that is now done at much expense and trouble at South Easton. The grading of the grounds has been commenced and will be prosecuted as vigorously as circumstances will permit. The foundation for a repair and erecting shop, 168 by 251 feet, has been laid and the walls are partly up; a building, 41 by 84 feet, for stationary engine and machine shop is under roof; and an engine house to accommodate 16 locomotives will be commenced in the spring. A good supply of water is to be had on the premises without pumping and a large tank has already been put up.

At South Easton an extension of the machine shop, 60 by 150 feet, two stories high, of stone, has been put under roof, and additional accommodations built for 8 engines. This completes the roundhouse and provides stalls for 27 locomotives. A lot of ground was purchased at Lehighton and a very convenient station house of brick for the accommodation of both passengers and freight erected thereon.

The station house at Slatington was completed early in the year. This, as well as that at Lehighton, gives very general satisfaction to the citizens and travelling public. I trust that ere the close of another year good and sufficient station houses will be built at Mauch Chunk, Bethlehem and Easton. At the latter place it is proposed to change the site of the depot to a point nearer South Easton, thereby accommodating both towns and placing the buildings in a less objectionable situation.

Three first class freight engines have been added to the rolling stock during the past year and three more have been ordered, all to be delivered by July of next year.

There have been built at our shops 62 eight wheel iron-truck coal cars, 31 iron-truck flat cars and 100 four wheel coal cars, and there were purchased from E. A. Packer & Co. 274 four wheel coal cars.

The equipment of the road now consists of 29 locomotives of all classes, 703 eight wheel coal cars, 874 four wheel coal cars, 77 flat cars, 8 passenger cars and 4 baggage cars. Contracts have been made for 1,000 four wheel coal cars, 50 flat cars and 2 passenger cars, all of which are to be delivered by the first of April, 1864. Contracts have also been made for a sufficient quantity of timber for 100 flat cars and about 500 coal cars.

The furnaces and rolling mills erected in the valley during the past year have had the effect of increasing the amount of coal used on the line of the road, about 49 per cent. This will probably be still further augmented, as additional furnaces and mills are building. The multiplication of manufacturing establishments in our valley not only increases the consumption of coal, but adds leargely to the other branches of our business, as is shown by our increased receipts from passengers and freight. A year ago it was confidently expected that both the Schuylkill Haven and Lehigh Railroad and the Penn Haven and White Haven Railroad would ere this have been contributing their quota of coal and other business from the Schuylkill and Wyoming regions. The former, after being prosecuted vigorously for a few months passed into the control of the Reading Railroad Company, who immediately suspended all operations thereon. The latter was much delayed in consequence of the great scarcity and high price of labor. The graduation and masonry is now in such a state of forwardness as to insure its completion in February next. Most of the cross-ties, and part of the iron, chairs and spikes have been delivered, and track laying commenced. There has been expended upon the work to date:

For graduation, masonry, cross-ties & engineering. $264,997 78
" Real estate............................ 1,350 00
" Railroad iron......................... 26,687 42

$293,035 20

Early in the fall a corps of engineers was put in the field to ascertain the feasability of a railroad line from the top of Wilkesbarre Mountain at Solomon's Gap, running west to the coal fields of Hanover and Newport Townships. A good route was got with grades of about 90 feet per mile against the trade. The grade is heavy, though but little, if any, more than that of the Delaware, Lackawanna and Western, while the elevation to be overcome is 300 feet less than via Scranton. A good location for inclined planes was found about two miles west of those of the Lehigh Coal and Navigation Company. It may be desirable to go still further west with the planes, though no examinations have yet been made to ascertain if suitable ground could be had. The coal designed to be reached has been almost entirely undeveloped and may probably remain so for some time unless the road in contemplation is built. When done it will increase the amount of tonnage from Wyoming Valley via the Lehigh route and should, therefore, be looked upon favorably by the various companies composing the lines to market.

The Lehigh and Mahanoy Railroad was formally opened to Mahanoy City on the first of September, since which time 9,046 tons of coal passed over it to the Lehigh Valley Railroad; about equal to the tonnage of our road during the corresponding months of 1855. It is hoped that the increase from Mahanoy in the coming eight years may keep pace with that of the Lehigh Valley during the past eight. In November its extension to Centralia was put under contract, making a main line from Catawissa Junction of 20 miles, with three branches of about 2½ miles each; all of which but about 4 miles is within the coal measures. There remain about 4 miles to build in addition to that now being graded to reach Mount Carmel, where it will connect with the Mount Carmel and Sunbury Railroad, thus forming a continuous rail communication between the Lehigh at Penn Haven and the Susquehanna at Sunbury. Its completion cannot fail to bring a very large tonnage to the Lehigh Valley and its southern and eastern connections.

The Lehigh Coal and Navigation Company are building a railroad from their chutes to connect with our road at the iron bridge, one mile below Mauch Chunk, with a view of shipping coal from their mines during the close of navigation.

The Catasauqua and Fogelsville Railroad Company are extending their road some eight miles to reach the magnetic ore beds of the Lehigh Mountain. If this deposit prove as rich and extensive as anticipated it will cheapen the manufacture of iron and thereby tend to increase the quantity produced in the vicinity.

The Bethlehem Railroad, extending from Bethlehem to Bath, is under contract and the grading now in progress. This road will also open fine deposits of iron ore, limestone and slate and will concentrate the trade and travel of that section of country upon our road at Bethlehem. Extensive slate quarries are now worked in the vicinity of Bath, the product of which is hauled to Easton for shipment.

Every year adds to the number of our connections, each one of which contributes more or less to our general business and prosperity; all should be encouraged and every facility offered for the prompt interchange of business by which we will be mutually benefitted.

It is gratifying to again bear testimony to the faithfulness and diligence of the heads of the various departments of transportation, construction and repairs and to the employees generally.

Very respectfully yours,
ROBT. H. SAYRE,
Superintendent and Engineer.

www.ingramcontent.com/pod-product-compliance
Lightning Source LLC
Chambersburg PA
CBHW020314090426
42735CB00009B/1343